DWARFS

A WARHAMMER ARMIES SUPPLEMENT

CONTENTS

Written by
Pete Haines

Additional Material
Rick Priestley

Cover Art
Paul Dainton

Illustration
Alex Boyd, Paul Dainton,
Wayne England, Karl Kopinski,
Adrian Smith & Sam Wood

Graphic Design
Alun Davies, Neil Hodgson
& Nuala Kinrade

Miniatures Design
Tim Adcock, Colin Grayson,
Mark Harrison, Alex Hedström,
Aly Morrison, Felix Paniagua
& Seb Perbet

Production
Michelle Barson, John Michelbach,
Mark Owen, Dylan Owen,
Ian Strickland & Nathan Winter

Hobby Material
Mark Jones & Adrian Wood

'Eavy Metal
Fil Dunn, Pete Foley, Neil Green,
Neil Langdown, Darren Latham,
Keith Robertson, Anya Wettergren
& Kirsten Williams

Special Thanks To....
Alessio Cavatore, Graham Davey,
Mark Gibbons, Asger Granerud,
Nick Kyme, Alan Merrett,
Anthony Reynolds, Gil Surepi,
Gav Thorpe & The Geeks

PRODUCED BY GAMES WORKSHOP

UK
Games Workshop Ltd.,
Willow Rd, Lenton,
Nottingham,
NG7 2WS

US
Games Workshop Inc.,
6721 Baymeadow Drive,
Glen Burnie,
Maryland 21060-6401

Canada
Games Workshop,
2679 Bristol Circle,
Unit 3, Oakville,
Ontario, L6H 6Z8

Australia
Games Workshop,
23 Liverpool Street,
Ingleburn
NSW 2565

ISBN: 1-84154-690-9   www.games-workshop.com   Product code: 60 03 02 05 003

INTRODUCTION

To the east of the Empire are the Worlds Edge Mountains. Here, between the so-called civilised lands of Men and the desolated regions of the Dark Lands, are the ancestral holds of one of the most ancient races of the Warhammer world – the Dwarfs. Their domains were once greater, but woe betide anyone who talks of decline in the company of a Dwarf! Karaz Ankor (as they call their realm) remains as resolute and unyielding as ever. In these dark times the Dwarfs are a bastion of honour, strength and courage in a world assailed by Chaos.

On the battlefield, the Dwarfs are known for their stubborn courage. Fighting on foot in close formation, clad in finely crafted mail and armed with superbly forged deadly axes, they are the most resolute and determined of warriors. They are also the most inventive folk in the world. Dwarfs have mastered the art of making black powder, learned the secrets of steam and a dozen other crafts that are a mystery to the rest of the world. This creativity is manifest in the many and varied war machines they bring to battle with them. From time-honoured Grudge Throwers and Bolt Throwers, to proven Cannons, to the more esoteric Organ Guns, Flame Cannon and Gyrocopters, no army has such powerful machinery.

Before an opponent can smash himself against the unyielding shield wall of the Dwarfs, he must first brave the bombardment of cannon balls, boulders and bolts rained down upon him by the Dwarf machines then, as he gets closer, bullets and quarrels are added to the storm. Finally, they must face the Dwarfs themselves, warriors as fierce and vengeful as they are skilled. There are few things in the world that frighten a Dwarf – and none they would admit to – so their enemies had best be prepared for a long, hard fight, for a Dwarf army will often stand and fight to the death rather than retreat and concede defeat.

The Dwarfs remember their friends and their enemies equally well. They stick to their word, even when honouring a pledge leads them to war, and as a consequence are a greatly valued ally. Once someone has made an enemy of a Dwarf, however, they have made an enemy not just for their own life but for the lives of their descendants as well. The Dwarfs do not forget grudges, indeed they harbour them, recording the slights and wrongdoings in great volumes. They do this so each affront can, in the course of time, be avenged.

A Dwarf army presents rank upon rank of bearded, mail-clad warriors with bright shields identifying their holds, clans, guilds and gods. As such, once you have mastered the techniques for painting mail and beards, you can approach painting a Dwarf army with confidence. For the more experienced modeller, Dwarf engines provide more of a challenge and give the army its centrepieces.

WHAT'S IN THIS BOOK

The History of the Dwarfs
Recounting the Dwarf history from their arrival in the Old World to the present day.

The Dwarf Realms
In which the mighty holds of the Dwarfs throughout the Old World are described.

Dwarf Society
Wherein we explain the culture of the Dwarfs, their realms and their grudges.

The Dwarf Throng
This section explains the background of the troops making up the Dwarf army, along with all the rules needed to use them in games of Warhammer.

Forces of the Dwarfs
A detailed army list specifies exactly what troops you can include in your army and provides the characteristic profiles for all the troop types.

Collecting a Dwarf army
This section shows how to begin collecting and painting your army. It explains how to represent different holds whilst still giving each Dwarf warrior a distinctive look. In addition, the 'Eavy Metal team has provided a showcase of some of the best painted miniatures in the world to inspire you to greater efforts.

On our web site you will find extra advice on collecting, painting and using the Dwarfs:

www.games-workshop.com

THE DWARFS

The Dwarfs are one of the most ancient races of the Warhammer world. From the beginning of time, their traditional homeland has been the Worlds Edge Mountains, the vast, forbidding mountain chain that marks the eastern boundary of the Old World. Here in ages past, the Dwarfs built their massive underground strongholds among the high peaks and tumbling chasms. At its height, their realm spread from the far north to the distant south, while their mines stretched far beneath the earth itself. These days of glory are now long gone; many strongholds lie in ruins or are occupied by evil creatures, and the great achievements of the past are now nothing more than memories, ancient sagas sung in the half-empty halls of the few surviving Dwarf strongholds.

Dwarfs are the greatest miners and tunnellers in the world, delving deep beneath their mountain homes for metals, precious stones and other mineral wealth buried there. From this raw material they make all kinds of precious objects, including weapons and armour, marvellous vessels and jewels worked with incredible skill. Beneath each Dwarf stronghold there exists a labyrinth of caverns and tunnels created and enlarged over centuries as the Dwarfs dug ever deeper in search of new riches.

Dwarfs are supremely skilled craftsmen and take great pride in everything they do. It is almost impossible for a Dwarf to hurry his work, and no Dwarf could ever bring himself to produce something slipshod or cheap. Whether it be forging weapons and armour, the construction of fortifications or the mechanical inventions of the famed Engineers Guild, the ingenuity and technical ability of Dwarfs is unsurpassed anywhere in the Old World. No other race, not even the great craftsmen of the High Elves, can rival the care and skill of the Dwarfs.

Dwarfs obtain all they really need by trading raw materials and artefacts with their neighbouring peoples. A few basic crops are grown within the walls of the Dwarf strongholds and hardy livestock graze on the high pastures. Good land is scarce in the mountains and Dwarfs are not great farmers, although they are enthusiastic hunters, able to find meat and fur even in the highest peaks. Grain and fruit are brought into the mountains by merchants and exchanged in the strongholds for metalwork and gold. If trade routes are cut by war and the strongholds are besieged, the dour Dwarfs tighten their belts and dine on Dwarf stone bread, a tough bread baked from a mixture of wild grain and pulverised rock, made almost palatable when washed down with good Dwarf ale! Indeed, Dwarf ale is so nourishing that Dwarfs can survive for weeks on this alone. Every stronghold has a great store of barrels and takes immense pride in the efficacy and unique flavour of its ale.

AGE, WEALTH AND SKILL

Dwarfs are a grim and exceptionally proud people. They are sparing with their praise and often disparaging about the achievements of other races. Dwarfs respect three things above all others: age, wealth and skill. Of course, a Dwarf will always carefully explain how his race is the oldest of all, how his ancestors earned unimaginable wealth, and how the Dwarfs are the most skilled builders and smiths in the world. This is not boasting, it is just setting the record straight.

Unless slain in battle, or some other mishap befalls them, Dwarfs live to a very great age. The relative length and fullness of a Dwarf's beard indicate how old and wise he is,

hence Dwarfs are immensely proud of their beards and never cut or trim them. Whatever they are doing, if Dwarfs are in any doubt as to how to proceed, they look to the Dwarf with the longest beard to tell them what to do. This is invariably the wisest solution.

Dwarfs have a great reverence for old things, valuing them for their memories and associations. When a skilled Dwarf smith dies, his work lives after him and forms a tangible connection to the past. The preservation and continuing use of some ancient device or construction is a form of respect and veneration for its creator. All Dwarf master craftsmen are adept at reforging ancient weapons or incorporating ancient relics into their new works.

Hoarding wealth is a great passion among Dwarfs. They are an industrious race and work hard for their riches and possessions. When a Dwarf dies, his possessions are divided amongst his family and so are passed on from generation to generation. A family's treasure is held most dear as it is both a source of wealth and a link between the living and the dead. No Dwarf feels secure unless his treasure hoard is heaped high enough for him to sit on.

The hoards of some ancient Dwarf lords were of legendary proportions. Even today, the riches of the remaining Dwarf strongholds are a great attraction to Orcs, Goblins and other would-be conquerors, but the Dwarfs are extremely tough and their strongholds have mostly withstood the test of time.

Nevertheless, over the millennia, several great and proud strongholds have fallen to Orcs and other invaders, their populations dispersed and slain, and their hoards of gold and artefacts broken up and scattered across the world.

All Dwarfs have a rigid sense of honour, which is centred upon a bond or promise. If a Dwarf makes a deal he will remember it and keep to it, even if it costs him dearly to do so. A Dwarf will honour the word of an ancestor even if it was made centuries before. In turn, Dwarfs expect others to keep their word, and look to the families of oathbreakers for recompense.

It is the worst possible insult to break faith with a Dwarf; it is also a serious mistake. A broken bond will be remembered forever and inevitably avenged. Great breaches of faith against the Dwarf people are recorded in a massive tome kept in Karaz-a-Karak, and known as the *Great Book of Grudges*. No dealings are entered into with anybody without prior reference to this book, which almost amounts to a chronicle of Dwarf history. It is part of Dwarf folklore and many Dwarfs know by heart its fiery accounts of great wrongs done to their ancestors.

Dwarfs have little knowledge of magic as it is practiced by Elves and Humans, and they have no wizards as such. The magical lore of the Dwarfs is closely linked to their craftsmanship in weaponry, armour and other artefacts. Dwarf Runesmiths make many magical devices, including the finest weapons and armour. They are masters of rune lore, the art of using runes to entrap magic and imbue artefacts with arcane power. Their knowledge has been passed down by word of mouth from the days of the ancestors, although knowledge of the most potent runes is a very powerful secret known to only a few of the most adept Runelords.

A DWARF HISTORY

The Dwarf strongholds of the Worlds Edge Mountains are remnants of the once great Dwarf empire known by the Dwarfs as Karaz Ankor. This means either the 'Everlasting Realm' or the 'Mountain Realm', the Dwarf word for mountain and extreme durability being the same. The great city of Karaz-a-Karak, called Everpeak in the tongue of Men, lay at the centre of this vast empire. The history of the Everlasting Realm is a long saga of war, treachery and betrayal that has left a bitter legacy in the minds of the Dwarf people.

The first Dwarfs migrated northward from their ancestral homelands in the southern part of the Worlds Edge Mountains. This all happened so long ago that it is impossible to say exactly when the Dwarfs began their journey or how long it took them to reach the lands they now inhabit. Their progress was probably a slow one as they followed veins of ore northwards, mining out the exposed seams and moving onwards in search of gold, iron, gemstones, and workable stone. As they progressed, they left clans scattered throughout the Worlds Edge Mountains. In the most ancient times, the Dwarfs lived in crude caves and fashioned stone tools from flint. Then, as now, they were a tough hardy folk, and they thrived and multiplied in the bleak inhospitable lands.

As the Dwarfs spread through the Worlds Edge Mountains they founded a system of strongholds. A stronghold is really a small realm centred around a fortified mine. Most strongholds lay over an especially productive seam or source of precious gems. Eventually, the Dwarfs reached the northernmost part of the Worlds Edge Mountains, a desolate region scattered with the bleached bones of many creatures. They called this cold, barren land Zorn Uzkul, or the 'Great Skull Land'.

From the Great Skull Land, many Dwarfs turned back south, daunted by the cold and the sparsity of mineral wealth. Others turned west into the land of Norsca where they settled amongst the cold mountains there, while some travelled east across the Great Skull Land and entered the Mountains of Mourn. For a while, these widely dispersed Dwarf kindreds maintained contact with each other, but soon they would be separated by the coming of Chaos.

THE COMING OF CHAOS

According to one account in the Great Book of Grudges, the most ancient of all Dwarf books of lore, the coming of Chaos rent the earth and sky, and tore the very mountains apart. The skies darkened and turbulent winds of multi-coloured magic clouded the air. It was evident that something terrible was occurring. The Dwarfs watched the skies, uncertain as to what was going to happen.

The Dwarfs maintain that it was Grungni himself who warned the Dwarfs of the coming of Chaos and showed them how to delve deep beneath the mountains. There, in the dark beneath the world, they took shelter as the winds of magic scoured the earth. In their wake, the winds left clouds that settled into a layer of fine black warp dust which mutated and corrupted everything it touched. The Dwarfs huddled

in their mines and caves as everything on the surface was tainted by chaos. Eventually the dreadful tempest passed and the Dwarfs emerged once more into daylight. They found the world had changed. Terrifying monsters roamed the mountains and daemons stalked the land in daylight.

The Dwarfs were not defenceless. The ancient tales tell how Grungni taught them how to inscribe magical runes onto their weapons and armour. He armed Grimnir with two mighty axes and armour harder than the bones of mountains. From their underground strongholds, the armies of the Dwarfs sallied forth to do battle against the hordes of Chaos. Valaya protected the Dwarfs against the dark magic of their enemies, and Grimnir slew many daemons with his axes. They did not have the numbers to turn back the tide but at least they kept their mountain realms clear of the monstrous servants of Chaos.

THE ORPHANS

The Dwarfs that had crossed the Great Skull Land were not so well defended. Their delvings were nowhere near as deep as the older holds in the Worlds Edge Mountains and no Grimnir, Grungni or Valaya arose to lead them, or at least no heroes have been recorded. The corruption of these Dwarfs into Chaos Dwarfs is a consistent omission in otherwise complete Dwarfen histories. All that is recorded is that around this time the family trees of the most ancient clans were all amended in some way. Clans with ancestors who had gone east were now 'adopted' as orphans by clans that remained behind. Clans whose sons had marched east no longer recognised that they had kin at all. Although many Dwarfs claim descent from the Ancestor Gods, the disruption caused in clan records at this time makes it very difficult to be sure about lineages dating back beyond this point. The

Dwarfs have kept their silence on the Orphan clans and it is still considered a grave insult to even mention the Chaos Dwarfs in their presence.

THE ELVES

It was during the war against Chaos that the Dwarfs first made contact with the Elves. A fleet of Elf warships, captained by Caledor Dragontamer, had been blown off course after a sea battle. This great Elf mage had searched the coasts of the Old World hoping to find clues to the source of the Chaos that was destroying the world. The Elves encountered a Dwarf army, led by Grimnir himself, that had been drawn into the lowlands while chasing a band of Chaos marauders.

It was a great moment in the history of both races as one of the greatest and most subtle High Elf mages of all time met the brutal and mighty incarnate Ancestor God of the Dwarf people. What Grimnir made of the tall and haughty Elf mage is not recorded, and what the Elf thought of the tattooed Dwarf warlord is also unknown. However, both realised that they were not enemies. The matter was settled when a mighty force of Beastmen arrived and was promptly smashed by Grimnir's axes and Caledor's spells. The following alliance of Elves and Dwarfs would save the world and then all but destroy these two proud races.

From Caledor, the Dwarfs learned of the great Phoenix King Aenarion and his struggle to free the distant land of Ulthuan from the grip of Chaos. From Grimnir, Caledor learned of the storm from the north that had preceded the coming of Chaos. Caledor realised that a Chaos Gate had opened in the uttermost north, a doorway between this world and the unimaginable daemonic realms of Chaos. Now Chaos had a foothold in the world and would quickly overwhelm its inhabitants.

With this information, Caledor returned to Ulthuan. Probably he was already hatching the plan that would lead to the creation of a mighty vortex to suck the unleashed chaos power out of the world. Upon Caledor's departure, Grimnir presented him with a runic amulet of sovereign protective power. In return, Caledor gifted the Dwarf with the Crystal of Fire that is kept to this day in the great vault of Karaz-a-Karak.

THE DOOM OF GRIMNIR

The Dwarfs continued to fight valiantly against the tides of Chaos. Having heard Caledor's description of the Chaos Gate, Grimnir decided to take more direct action. Ignoring the advice of Grungni and Valaya, he decided to trek north and close the gate himself, little imagining what cosmic energies he would encounter. Grungni told him he would surely die but Grimnir snarled that it was worth the risk. He shaved his head and beard save for one crest of hair that ran from the nape of his neck to his forehead. Grimnir gave one of his axes to his son, Morgrim, and departed for the north, chanting his death song. Morgrim followed him to the very edge of the wastes that lay around the north, ignoring his father's commands to turn back. In the end, he respected his father's wishes and watched his mighty sire fade into the shimmering haze of the poisoned land.

Grimnir was never seen again, and no one knows what befell this valiant Dwarf. Perhaps he was pulled down by an army of monsters. One tale says that he fought his way to the mouth of the gate and held it against an army of Daemons even as Caledor opened his vortex on Ulthuan. Perhaps a stranger and more terrible doom overtook him. Of the fate of Grimnir the Dwarfs do not speak. They say only that he fell in darkness long ago. His axe was lost with him.

THE GOLDEN AGE

In the end, Caledor was successful in his attempt to create the vortex and the armies of Chaos were driven back to lurk in the shadowy corners of the world. Grungni and Valaya vanished. Some say they returned to the mountains' heart where they were created and will re-emerge some day. In the Worlds Edge Mountains the Dwarfs prospered as never before, but of their kin in the far north they heard no word. During this age, mighty strongholds were built around the cores of the old fortresses and a vast network of underground highways was built to link them together.

Trade was established with the Elves as they returned to the Old World to build their colonies along the coasts and in the woods. It was during this time that all the great Dwarf cities were founded. A long age of peace and prosperity ensued, which was to last for nearly a thousand years.

In Karaz-a-Karak, the Dwarf High King sat upon his carved throne and presided over the Dwarf Lords who ruled the other great strongholds. This was the great age of the Dwarfs when, in friendship with the Elves, they explored the Old World for its riches. Trade flourished between these two ancient peoples and they lived side by side in the trading ports and cities of the Old World. At this time, Men were divided into primitive tribes, eager to learn from older and wiser races.

Elves and Dwarfs were perhaps not as wise as Men had believed, for Elf arrogance and Dwarf obstinacy led to friction and eventually outright war. A terrible long slaughter began which lasted for an entire age.

The Dwarfs put the blame for the war on the fickleness of Elven friendship. So great were the works of the Dwarfs, so prized for their craftsmanship and ingenuity, that the Elves became jealous and avaricious. The first acts of the war were attacks on Dwarf trading caravans that slaughtered beardlings and maids, as well as warriors. Evidence was found that Elves were responsible and hastily organised pursuit brought some of the perpetrators to summary justice.

The High King, Gotrek Starbreaker was a prudent and wise lord, as could be seen by his beard, and not given to hasty action. He halted any further war-making by his thanes and sent envoys to far Ulthuan to resolve the dispute peacefully and honourably. Tales tell of how they were greeted with contempt and scorn. The arrogant Elves deliberately conceived of an insult so grievous that it could only result in war most terrible and a grudge that would be passed from Dwarf father to son down the ages. The envoys were shaved of their beards. Humiliated beyond endurance, the envoys were expelled from the Elf lands and compelled to return home, across the lands of strangers, without their beards or their pride.

There could be but one response: war! Even so, the Dwarfs did not completely yield to anger, but made their preparations well, Throughout the realm the workshops laboured night and day to make ancient war machines ready for battle and put a new edge on heirloom axes. Provisions were drawn in so that each hold could withstand a siege if need be. Finally, when all was ready, the warhorns sounded from the high towers of every hold and the High King sent for his warriors. From every corner of the empire, kings mustered their throngs (as Dwarf armies are known) and marched to the call of the High King. Every Dwarf was harnessed in the finest mail and each axe bore a favoured rune or three. Each army was accompanied by the finest war engines of the day: powerful Bolt Throwers, easily capable of shattering the flimsy toys of the Elves, and ancient Grudge Throwers, their missiles engraved with every just grievance, ready to be hurled at the spindly towers of the Elves, and bring them crashing down for their affront. Never before or since has such a sight been seen; the full might of the Dwarfs at the height of their power.

Perhaps the sons of Grungni and Grimnir were overconfident in their power. In the early clashes, Snorri Halfhand, the son of King Gotrek fought with Caledor, the Phoenix King himself. Such a deed was courageous to be sure, but Snorri had overreached himself. He lacked the wisdom to be ready for the trickery of the Elves and, drawn into personal combat with the most powerful Elf, was despatched by an underhand blow that an older Dwarf would have been wise to. Snorri's army fought well and slew many Elves, but were forced from the field.

The loss of Halfhand incensed Gotrek's kin. Morgrim, Snorri's cousin, fuelled by his rage and greed, marched on Oeragor. The Elves sought to avoid battle, fearing Morgrim's wrath but eventually, after two days of manoeuvring, they were brought to account. The battle was long, both sides firing upon each other for hours, the Dwarfs intent on proving they could withstand any arrow-storm the Elves could muster. Eventually, in desperation, the Elves closed to handgrips and the real slaughter began. Morgrim cut into the heart of the Elf host and fought his way to Imladrik, Prince of Ulthuan. In the name of Snorri Halfhand, Morgrim cut the Elfling in twain thereby earning the title of Elgidum or Elfdoom.

Even then neither side would relent. Years passed, each of them marked by great battles as the Elves and Dwarfs bled each other dry.

King Gotrek and his throng joined Morgrim in besieging the port citadel of Tor Alessi. Here the grudges were repaid in most literal fashion. Great rocks, bound in iron, rained on the Elf city for a hundred days. By this time, the walls were breached in a dozen places and not one tower remained to halt the advance. The Starbreaker and the Elgidum attacked together and

sought out the treacherous King Caledor. Unable to flee, Caledor was forced to face Gotrek and the two kings clashed in personal combat. Caledor sought swift victory but King Starbreaker denied him. The Dwarf king was content to fight on as day gave way to night and gradually, the Elf's fortitude began to fail him. Still Gotrek fought on, drawing the last reserves from his foe before shattering Caledor's light Elven sword with a well-placed hammer blow. Defeated utterly, Caledor pleaded for mercy but the High King carried the burden of vengeance for his people. Mercy was not his to give, merely justice, and so he ended King Caledor's life with a single blow of his hammer.

As proof of the victory and testament to a grudge settled, King Gotrek brought the crown of King Caledor home to Karaz-a-Karak where it was to remain to this day. The Elves withdrew from the Old World, their arrogance shattered by their defeat. Although the war was ended, the Dwarfs would never forget, and distrust of the Elves became the most common wisdom passed down the generations.

THE END OF THE GOLDEN AGE

The War of the Beard, as the War of Vengeance became known to the Elves, should have ensured the Dwarfs dominion over the Old World for ages to come. The fates were not kind, however, and before the Everlasting Realm could recover from the conflict, the Dwarfs were beset by natural disasters unparalleled since the first great Chaos incursion.

The end came amid earthquakes and volcanic eruptions along the entire length of the Worlds Edge Mountains. The great walls surrounding the strongholds were broken, the subterranean highways collapsed, and mine workings were shattered and flooded. Lava poured into the cavernous vaults beneath the Dwarf strongholds and the whole of the Everlasting Realm was thrown into disarray. In the wake of these natural disasters came hordes of Goblins, Orcs, Skaven and the vile followers of Chaos. They infiltrated the Dwarf tunnels and overwhelmed beleaguered outposts with surprise attacks from deep below the ground.

Karak Ungor was the first stronghold to fall, its caverns and halls becoming home to the Night Goblins. Karak Varn was shattered by an earthquake and soon after fell to the invaders. The mines at Ekrund were sacked by Orcs, driving the Dwarfs out of the Dragonback Mountains. The gold mines at Gunbad were taken by Night Goblins. Mount Silverspear was eventually lost to the Orcs, and the whole of the eastern fringe of the Worlds Edge Mountains was afterwards abandoned.

All over the Dwarfs' Everlasting Realm, small settlements, mines, and temples, were destroyed and occupied by their enemies, dividing and isolating the remaining Dwarf strongholds and changing the nature of the Dwarf lands forever.

THE GOBLIN WARS

For almost a thousand years the Dwarfs fought on, sometimes winning back their lost settlements for a while, at other times coming perilously close to destruction. Eventually, the growing strength of the Orcs and Goblins in the south led to the fall of almost all the Dwarf strongholds in the southern part of the Worlds Edge Mountains. Karak Eight Peaks fell after a desperate and protracted struggle in the vast network of tunnels and vaults beneath the great city. Karak Azgal was stormed and sacked, but its treasure horde was never found. The Orcs abandoned its vaults in anger, leaving the ruins to become a nest for dragons and its catacombs the lair of monsters. Karak Drazh was attacked and captured, becoming the Orc fortress of Black Crag. After a thousand years of resistance, the Dwarfs lost three strongholds within a space of fifty years.

Following this second reversal in its fortunes, the once glorious Dwarf empire lay shattered and in ruins, its power broken forever, and its treasures scattered among the conquering hordes. Orcs and Goblins infested the great subterranean halls where Dwarf bards once recited their heroic sagas. Trolls desecrated the tombs of kings and gnawed upon their bones. Foetid Skaven scuttled through the catacombs and passages spreading disease and decay. The Dwarfs grimly held onto their surviving strongholds and honed their axes in bitterness.

This was the time when many Dwarfs forsook their ancient homeland and wandered westward into the Grey Mountains where they built new and prosperous strongholds, though naturally these could never rival the great works of their ancestors. Indeed, at this time, there was some dispute between the Dwarfs determined to fight on for the lost holds whatever the cost and those willing to begin again elsewhere. Though this did not escalate into a conflict, hard words and a few blows were exchanged. No matter how the new holds prospered, there would always be a view that they were second best to the holds of the Worlds Edge Mountains.

At the time, however, there was no chance to reflect on this. Between the Grey Mountains and the Worlds Edge Mountains, the Dwarfs established new trade routes, or reopened routes used in the distant past when they traded with the Elves. The lands themselves were full of Orcs and Goblins, and the emerging tribes of Men who fought the Greenskins for possession of the land. The Dwarfs did all they could to encourage the Men, seeing in them a natural ally against the Orcs. Trade between the two races grew slowly, and the Dwarfs taught Mankind many of their lesser secrets such as how to work iron into weapons and armour. When the High King Kurgan Ironbeard was captured by Orcs, it was a man who rescued him – Sigmar, the mighty warrior founder of the Empire. This act forged a bond of friendship that has existed between Men and Dwarfs ever since, for Dwarfs never forget a debt, especially a debt incurred a long time ago.

It was at this time that the Dwarfs gifted Sigmar with the mighty rune hammer Ghal Maraz which was to become the symbol of the manling Emperors ever after.

Together, the Dwarfs and Sigmar's warriors drove the Orcs and Goblins from the western lands, and a new age of peace and prosperity began. Many Dwarfs moved into the Empire to set up as blacksmiths and traders amongst the growing Human settlements. There was plenty of work for Dwarf swordsmiths, for there were still many Greenskins left in the forests to find and drive out. Men could make good use of every sword the Dwarfs forged and would pay for them in gold.

The alliance of Dwarfs and the descendants of Sigmar has continued to the present day. The Dwarfs have fought long and hard to re-establish their supremacy over the mountains, but the Orcs and their evil allies do not give up their ground easily. Every cavern, tunnel and vault must be fought for and paid for in Dwarf blood. But Dwarfs forget nothing, and they will never let a hammer rest or lay an axe aside while their ancestors are dishonoured, and their tombs desecrated.

THE CHAOS WARS

Men, although much more dependable than Elves, are short-lived and possessed of an unquenchable thirst for glory and power. Properly harnessed, such feelings were noble and courageous, but gradually Men became aware of an easier, altogether more seductive path to greatness: the path of Chaos. The Dwarfs gave warning of the danger, knowing how close Chaos had come to consuming the entire world in death and madness in the past. Wise men heeded them but many did not, and with a ready supply of supplicants the Dark Powers grew strong again. The Men of Norsca, the Kurgan and, in the east, the Hung, barbaric peoples all, fell under the influence of Chaos and their Champions looked at the civilised lands beyond the Worlds Edge Mountains with rapacious hunger.

Even in the Empire, where Sigmar had established a fine realm, the power of Chaos waxed strong. The Empire was respected by the Dwarfs, knowing it to be built around their gifts, notably the hammer Ghal Maraz and the twelve Runefang swords, used by Men to identify the Emperor and the Elector Counts who ruled beneath

him. But, in the forests, Men tainted and mutated by Chaos grew in strength and the reach of the Emperor did not extend far beyond the gates of his cities.

Eventually, raiding turned to open war and the hordes of Chaos surged through the High Pass and down from Norsca, filling the Troll Country with marching armies. The port of Erengrad fell, as did the great city of Praag, amidst horrors undreamt of by Men and recalled only in ancient nightmares by Dwarfs. It seemed that the Empire might fall before the onslaught but Dwarfs do not forget their oaths. High King Alriksson raised his banner alongside that of the Emperor-to-be, Magnus the Pious. Together they raised the siege of Kislev, sundering the Chaos horde and sending it scuttling and slithering back to the Northern Wastes.

There could be no celebration though, for what Chaos touches is rarely the same again. The city of Praag was testament to this. Even after the tide of Chaos recoiled, what was left was a place of dread that could never be restored to its original grandeur. Although Men gave thanks to their god, for that is how they saw young Sigmar now, the Dwarfs grumbled in their beards that the worst was yet to come and that Chaos would return, though it would be many generations of Men before it came to pass.

They were right. Beyond the civilised lands, in the Chaos Wastes, a mighty Warlord arose, Archaon the Everchosen was his name. He was favoured by the Dark Gods, at least insofar as blood greed and madness was a blessing, and at his command a new storm began to gather that would eclipse anything that had gone before.

BATTLE OF EAST GATE

The loss of Karak Eight Peaks, the most ancient and magnificent of their holds, was a bitter blow to the Dwarfs. When Lord Belegar recaptured the citadel, it was seen as an opportunity to retake the entire hold. Belegar's kinsman, Lord Duregar of Karaz-a-Karak answered the call. Defeating an Orc force in the Battle of the Jaws, Duregar's army marched through Death Pass to the East Gate of Karak Eight Peaks. Their way was barred by a well-garrisoned watchtower and, as they advanced on it, Goblin hordes swept down on them from either side of the valley and Orcs closed the valley behind them.

The Dwarf advance was first slowed, then halted, by the sheer numbers of Night Goblins that confronted them. Despite inflicting massive casualties on the Goblins, the Dwarfs were being inexorably dragged down by the enemy hordes and had no choice but to take up a

defensive position on a low rise and chant their death songs. When all seemed lost, the East Gate exploded and through the smoke and ruin the army of Belegar sallied out. The Night Goblins, confused and outflanked, wavered for the first time and, seizing the moment, Belegar's army forced its way to Duregar's force. Together, the Dwarf armies marched back through the gate and on to the relative safety of the citadel of Karak Eight Peaks, fighting off further Greenskin attacks every pace of the way.

Rarely have such overwhelming odds been overturned; this victory is a testament to Dwarfen courage and discipline. Although the Dwarf enclave in Karak Eight Peaks remains small, the victory at East Gate allowed many treasures to be rescued and moved to safety elsewhere.

High King Thorgrim Grudgebearer ruled in Karaz-a-Karak and brought the strength and sureness of tradition back to the Dwarfs. Thorgrim settled grudges as other Dwarfs empty tankards. Even before he became king, he led expeditions into the lost holds, most notably recovering the Sceptre of Norgrim from Karak Eight Peaks. As king he energised the Dwarf people and set an example that the other Dwarf kings could not help but follow. King Ranulfsson of Karak Hirn followed the High King's lead with considerable success and even in worldly Barak Varr, King Byrrnoth presided over a return to traditional values. Thorgrim's rule has reminded the Dwarfs that, although they no longer held the power they once did, they were still a force in the world. It was fortunate for the Empire that such a strong king ruled among the Dwarfs.

When Chaos struck, Archaon's attack was aimed at the Empire city of Middenheim. Once again the Dwarfs honoured their oaths to Men and rallied to fight Chaos, just as their Ancestor Gods had millennia before. Ungrim Ironfist, the Slayer King of Karak Kadrin, led his orange-crested warriors to battle against the hordes of Vardek Crom, the Herald of Archaon.

Meantime Ungrim's son Garagrim, who had taken up the Slayer Oath in his father's stead, was determined to take the fight to the enemy. Reaching Praag, Garagrim met his avowed doom, slaying a monstrous Chaos Giant and achieved the death in battle that his oath demanded.

His father held Peak Pass against numerous attacks but when the forces of the Chaos Dwarfs entered the conflict, he was unable to hold any longer. Hearing of the death of Garagrim, Ungrim took upon himself the Slayer Oath once again, thereby merging his oath as king and his oath to seek death.

At the gates of Middenheim, the greatest armies of the age clashed. The events of that battle are well known, for the world did not fall to Archaon. Suffice to say that at the forefront of the armies of Men was the Exalted of Sigmar, Valten, armed now with Ghal Maraz and clad in the fine gromril armour presented to him by Barak Grimjaw. The first blows to fall on Archaon had in fact been struck centuries earlier, when forging the mighty rune hammer as a gift for the God of the Empire.

Such are the lessons of the ages and none know them so well as the Dwarfs. There will be no respite – numberless Skaven and Goblins will always press in on their realm but Dwarfs will still honour their oaths and their traditions and stand fast in the face of whatever enemies dare to cross steel with them.

DEEDS OF THE AGES

The Dwarfs invented their runic script long ago and have used it to make exacting records of their discoveries and dealings ever since. Each stronghold has always maintained its own library of history, written by scribes and concerned mostly with the affairs of that particular stronghold. Over the years, some of these huge books have been lost, or badly damaged, but even so the history of the Dwarfs is extremely long and thoroughly documented compared to that of the tribes of Men. Of particular importance is the Great Book of Grudges in Karaz-a-Karak, which is basically a record of long-standing vendettas. The Great Book of Grudges (Dammaz Kron in Dwarfish) is merely one of many books of this kind, for every stronghold keeps its own Book of Grudges. Every Dwarf clan and guild has its own too, and even families often keep written records of ancient disputes with their neighbours. The wealth of historical detail these books contain is enormous and far too great to be summarised in any detail here. The following historical overview describes only a limited selection of important events, or events which have been considered of particular interest. The Dwarfs employ a recording system based on the founding of Karaz-a-Karak, but dates from the more commonly used Imperial Calendar are given in the following descriptions.

Imperial Year

-4500 The Time of the Ancestor Gods. No written records of these times survive but legend relates that the Dwarfs began their slow colonisation of the Worlds Edge Mountains about the Imperial year -5000. This age came to a close with the coming of Chaos, the disappearance of the Ancestor God Grimnir into the Chaos Wastes, and the disappearance of the other Ancestor Gods shortly afterwards. Dwarf tradition holds that Grimnir closed the mighty Chaos Gate after battling with the Chaos gods, thereby saving the world from certain doom. Shortly before Grimnir's disappearance, the Dwarfs and High Elves meet for the first time, and friendly relations are established between the two races.

-4119 In this year, Malekith of the High Elves and Snorri Whitebeard, the High King of the Dwarfs, combine their mighty armies and finally drive out the last remnants of Chaos from the Old World. Afterwards, trade between the Dwarfs and Elves flourishes and the Dwarfs found many new strongholds.

-2839 The High Elf Phoenix King Bel-Shanaar visits the newly founded Dwarf stronghold of Karaz-a-Karak where he is made welcome by the venerable Snorri Whitebeard. The two great kings swear an oath of friendship, and Malekith remains in Karaz-a-Karak as his king's ambassador. For a while, Elves and Dwarfs prosper, until the Elves are drawn back to Ulthuan where civil strife is tearing their land apart.

-2188 After many centuries, the Elves return once more to the Old World. The Dwarfs learn of the civil war amongst the Elves and the treachery of Malekith. The two races begin to trade once more. Bargains are struck and Dwarf craftsmanship reaches new heights of ambition and accomplishment.

-2005 The Great Betrayal mars relationships between Dwarfs and Elves. Dwarf traders are ambushed and murdered, Dwarf settlements are plundered and honest Dwarf craftsmen cheated of their gold. The Dwarfs believe the Elves are to blame. Their attackers are in fact Dark Elf raiders sent by Malekith to sow dissent between the two races. Many Elves are slain by Dwarf travellers believing themselves under attack. The Elves retaliate in kind. Soon both sides begin to muster their armies.

-2000 In this year, Elves come from over the sea and set up a fortress near Krag Bryn. Their deceitful ways ferment ill will between the Dwarfs of Krag Bryn and Kazad Thrund. Eventually, Queen Helgar Thrundsdottir and Drong the Hard unite, both in marriage and on the battlefield, to settle their grudges, although it cost Drong his life.

Karak Zorn, in the great mountains of the Southlands comes into conflict with the Lizardmen that dwell there. Little is heard of it hereafter.

-1997 Dwarf High King Gotrek Starbreaker sends an ambassador to Ulthuan in a last ditch attempt to prevent a war. Dwarf demands for fair recompense for Elf hostilities are met with arrogance and the ambassadors are thrown out. As a final insult, the Elves shave off their beards, and it is from this incident that the following war takes its Elf name of the War of the Beard. The Dwarfs, not a people to take such matters lightly, refer to the conflict as the War Against the Elves, or the War of Vengeance.

-1974 Snorri Halfhand, son of the High King, is slain by King Caledor II after challenging the Elf to single combat.

-1968 Morgrim, cousin of Snorri Halfhand, kills the Elf Lord Imladrik at the Battle of Oeragor.

-1948 The Elf city of Athel Maraya is burned to the ground by a Dwarf army led by Morgrim.

-1560 The Battle of Three Towers at the gates of Tor Alessi. The Dwarfs defeat the Elves in a cataclysmic battle for mastery of the Old World. Gotrek Starbreaker kills the Phoenix King Caledor II and takes the Phoenix Crown as recompense for the many wrongs suffered by his people. The High Elves abandon their cities and sail back to Ulthuan or retreat into the woods of Loren.

-1500 After the end of the War of Vengeance, the Dwarf Empire enjoys only a few years of peace before the Worlds Edge Mountains are riven by earthquakes and volcanic eruptions. The Dwarfs refer to this disaster and ensuing period of anarchy as the Time of Woes. The records of many strongholds are lost or disrupted for a time, and even the Great Book of Grudges in Karaz-a-Karak falls strangely silent. From what records remain, it is clear that many Dwarfs were slain and countless mines and small settlements destroyed. Even the larger holds were badly damaged as great rents opened in the earth and whole levels were swamped with molten lava. The Underway is partially ruined and blocked in many places, cutting the strongholds off from one another.

The following period is known as the time of the Goblin Wars, although if truth be known the Dwarfs' foes included Orcs, Ogres, Trolls, Skaven and all manner of other evil creatures. The first hold to fall is Karak Ungor in the Imperial year -1500. This hold is taken over by Night Goblins and known thereafter as Red Eye Mountain.

-1499 Karak Varn, already flooded when earthquakes split the rock apart allowing water into the lower workings, is destroyed by Skaven and Night Goblins.

-1498 The mines at Ekrund are seized by Orcs after months of heavy fighting by the vastly outnumbered Dragonback Dwarfs. In this year and afterwards, the watchtowers of Mad Dog Pass are abandoned or seized by Goblins.

-1457 The gold mines at Gunbad fall to the Night Goblins after many years of sporadic fighting. Gunbad was the largest and richest mine in the Worlds Edge Mountains and the unique source of brynduraz or brightstone – a brilliant blue crystal rock much valued by Dwarf craftsmen.

-1387 Beginning of the Silver Road Wars. Battle rages around Mount Silverspear, the richest remaining Dwarf mine.

-1367 Mount Silverspear is taken by the Orc Warlord Urk Grimfang who fortifies the mines still further and renames his conquest Mount Grimfang, a name it has borne ever since.

-1362 The Dwarfs abandon the last of their mines and smaller settlements in the eastern part of the Worlds Edge Mountains.

-1250 About this time the volcano Thunder Mountain, long quiet since the Time of Woes, erupts once more driving Orcs, Goblins and Trolls northwards. They attack Dwarf prospectors and miners. The settlements of Valhorn and Budrikhorn, south of Karaz-a-Karak, are destroyed by rampaging Trolls. The ensuing attempts to contain and drive out these creatures are known as the Troll Wars.

-1245 King Morgrim Blackbeard leads his forces southwards. After several pitched battles he drives away the Orcs and other evil creatures from the mountains north of Mad Dog Pass. Another Dwarf army led by Logazor Brightaxe heads east and succeeds in recapturing Mount Gunbad, but is forced to abandon the mines when Orc reinforcements arrive. Mount Silverspear is attacked by the Dwarfs, but the army is compelled to return westward when a horde of Trolls and Ogres moves towards Karaz-a-Karak. The horde is successfully repulsed from the Dwarf capital and the bodies of many Trolls are piled into a huge mound and burned.

-1190 Kadrin Redmane leaves Karak Varn in search of vengeance upon the swarms of Skaven that have soiled the tunnels of the hold.

-1185 An expedition led by Runesmith Kadrin Redmane clears the ruins of Karak Varn, driving the Skaven down into the deepest underhalls. He discovers a rich vein of gromril and petitions the High King to allow him to resettle the old stronghold. Miners flock to Karak Varn and gromril begins to flood into the High King's coffers.

-1136 Kadrin Redmane is ambushed and killed beside the shore of Black Water while leading a mule train of gromril ore to the High King. Kadrin slays thirty-six massive Orcs before he sustains a mortal wound and falls. His last act is to throw his rune hammer far out into the Black Water to prevent it falling into the hands of the enemy. Following Kadrin's death, the Dwarfs' hold on Karak Varn becomes increasingly tenuous, until they are eventually driven out by Skaven. Karak Varn once more falls into the hands of the Dwarfs' foes.

-975 Battle of a Thousand Woes. King Skorri Morgrimson leads a massive Dwarf army northwards in an attempt to recapture Karak Ungor. The Dwarfs clear their enemies from the southern valley and gate, but are ambushed and driven back when they attempt to enter the stronghold itself. A few Dwarfs, including Furgil, Skorri's youngest son, manage to infiltrate the lower halls, but they do not return. Skorri leads the remnants of his army back to Karaz-a-Karak and dies shortly afterwards.

-750 Karak Azgal is attacked by Goblins. They are repulsed after heavy fighting but go on to attack Karak Azul where they manage to gain a foothold in the western halls and lower regions. The Dwarfs continue to fight and slowly gain the upper hand, expelling the invaders only after many valiant defenders have been slain.

-650 Baragor, the first Slayer King, dedicates the great Shrine of Grimnir in Karak Kadrin. He takes the name of Ungrim, which means 'oath-bound' or 'unfulfilled oath'. His descendants bear the name to this day.

-513 The fall of Karak Eight Peaks. Over a period of more than a hundred years, the number of Goblins and Skaven have increased in and around the Dwarf stronghold until even daily life becomes a constant battle for survival. The Dwarfs find themselves driven into an ever diminishing realm as one after another of the eight peaks fall to the invaders. The end comes suddenly. Skaven poison the wells and use noxious gases to choke the Dwarfs. In the final moments, King Lunn orders his followers to rune-seal the tombs of the Kings of Old and the hold is abandoned. The King and remaining Dwarfs vow to return and one day reclaim their own.

-469 Karak Azgal is attacked and destroyed by Orcs and Goblins. Encouraged by their easy victory, the Greenskins move on to attack Karak Drazh. Karak Drazh falls after a long battle and is taken over by the Orcs and renamed Black Crag. Over the following years, the lands between Mad Dog Pass and Fire Mountain are taken over by Goblins, save for the Dwarf stronghold of Karak Azul. Karak Azul is besieged but holds out, the number of its defenders having been swollen by the influx of Dwarfs from the lost strongholds. This is a sad time for the Dwarfs. Many nurse bitter memories of defeat and humiliation.

-380 Orc Warlord Ugrok Beardburner leads the Orc hordes northwards and attacks Karaz-a-Karak. Many smaller settlements are destroyed, countless mines are overwhelmed and many Dwarfs die. The Dwarf High King, Logan Proudbeard, is captured by the Orcs and suffers great humiliation at the hands of his tormentors. Driven into a fury by the seizure of their King, the Dwarfs, led by Gorazin Silverhorn, finally drive the Orcs away from the capital. Orc armies continue to rampage throughout the Dwarf realms until the following year when the Orcs are defeated at the Battle of Black Water.

-250 About this time the Dwarfs intensify their trading contacts with the tribes of Men in the lands that are to become the Empire. Men are poor craftsmen and learn comparatively slowly.

-108 Daled Stormbreaker leads an expedition to recover the lost treasures of Karak Azgal.

-15 A trading convoy from Karaz-a-Karak is ambushed on its way to the Grey Mountains. King Kurgan Ironbeard is captured by the Orcs but is later rescued by Sigmar, prince of the Unberogen tribe. This is to prove a fortuitous event, for the friendship between Sigmar and Kurgan Ironbeard will blossom into the great alliance between the races of Dwarf and Men. In gratitude for his rescue, the Dwarf king gives Sigmar the rune hammer Ghal Maraz, an ancient heirloom of his clan.

-1   The Battle of Black Fire Pass. This battle is the culmination of a long campaign waged by the Dwarfs and Sigmar. The Greenskins are gradually driven from the lands west of the Worlds Edge Mountains and many Orcs and Goblins are destroyed or flee into the mountains. At the Battle of Black Fire Pass, a massive Orc army is destroyed by the combined forces of Sigmar and Kurgan Ironbeard, ending the domination of the land by the Orcs. Afterwards, Sigmar becomes the first emperor of a united Empire.

The creation of the Empire opens up a new age for the Dwarfs. Many Dwarfs travel to the Empire where they help the Humans build their first cities. Dwarf masons, carpenters and smiths are much in demand, and Dwarf workmanship is admired everywhere. As the Empire grows, the Dwarfs and Men establish valuable trading contacts and prosperity returns once more to the Dwarf realms. Dwarf and Human armies keep the Orcs and Goblins at bay. Several expeditions are mounted to reclaim lost strongholds, but none come to anything.

287   Dwarf miners discover the nest of the dragon Mordrak in the mountains south of Karak Azul.

657   Thori Gundrikson discovers gromril in the caves west of Black Water. The Dwarfs excavate substantial tunnels and extract great quantities of the ore over the following years. The mines are eventually destroyed by Skaven intruders, but not until the gromril is almost exhausted.

662   The discovery of the Lost Heartstone of Aldin Getgold in the Dragonback Mountains by Dorin Heldour and Katalin Kandoom.

684   The restoration of the Axe of Dail by Dorin Heldour and Katalin Kandoom. The axe is discovered deep in the ruins of Karak Varn and is recovered and brought back to King Finn Sourscowl in Karaz-a-Karak.

685   Dorin Heldour brings the skin of the dragon Fyrskar to Finn Sourscowl. Heganbor the Runesmith fashions the skin into a cloak engraved with potent runes.

742   Dorin Heldour and Katalin Kandoom rescue Elmador and Oldor Finnson from the dungeons of Black Crag. Elmador later becomes High King.

892   In this year, Kragg the Grimm forges the Rune of Stone under the eye of his master Morek Furrowbrow. He is to become the greatest and most long-lived Runesmith of his age.

1032   Skalf Dragonslayer slays the dragon Graug the Terrible and claims the kingship of Karak Azgal. The hold remains infested by Goblins, Skaven and other monsters, and the Dwarfs make no attempt to recapture it. Skalf and his descendants establish a town in the valley below the old entrance.

1111   The Black Plague sweeps the Old World. The Dwarfs seal their strongholds. The Skaven rise from the depths and attack the Dwarf strongholds in vast numbers, but the Dwarfs hold out despite many casualties.

1420   The lands around Karak Kadrin are tormented by the great dragon Skaladrak Incarnadine.

2010   The Battle of Hunger Wood. The Dwarfs fight many battles alongside the Empire in the Wars of the Vampire Counts. They take part in the Night Siege of Castle Tempelhof and the defeat of the Vampire Countess Emmanuelle.

2205   Battle of Black Falls. A Dwarf and Goblin army meet on the shores of the Black Water. Dwarf High King Alrik and Goblin Warlord Gorkil Eyegouger are slain while fighting along the rim of the Black Falls. The Goblin Warlord is mortally wounded by the Dwarf, but pulls his adversary to his doom over the falls. The Goblin army is routed into the icy water and most are swept over the falls and perish with their leader.

2302   The Great War Against Chaos. Chaos armies pour down from the north, devastating the lands as they come. Karaz-a-Karak is attacked but holds out. The Dwarfs send troops to Kislev, where Magnus the Pious lifts the siege.

2321   The Battle of Bloodwater Sound. After destroying the fleets of the Human realms, a Skaven fleet rampages along the coasts of the Old World looting and destroying. Dwarf Ironclads from Barak Varr seek out and defeat the Skaven in the Black Gulf.

2350   The Engineers' Guild Hall in Karaz-a-Karak is destroyed by explosions caused by Burlok Damminson and Sven Hasselfriesian's pressure vessel experiments.

2420   Goblin Warlord Grom rampages through the Worlds Edge Mountains, destroying tombs, mines and small settlements. Grom defeats a Dwarf army sent to oppose him at the Battle of Iron Gate before heading westward into the Empire.

2473   Belegar, descendant of King Lunn, declares himself king of Karak Eight Peaks having arrived there and set up camp on the site of the old citadel. What began as a treasure hunting expedition turns into an attempt to recolonise the hold. The Dwarfs descend into the depths and recover many treasures, but are hopelessly outnumbered and live in a state of permanent siege.

2498   Battle of the Jaws. A Dwarf army heading south to reinforce Karak Eight Peaks is attacked as it moves through Mad Dog Pass. The Dwarfs, led by Duregar, destroy the attacking Orcs and move southwards. The Dwarf army is ambushed once more at the Battle at the East Gate of Karak Eight Peaks, but fights its way through to the stronghold with heavy losses.

2503   Karak Azul is attacked by Orcs led by Gorfang Rotgut. Orcs get inside by means of a forgotten tunnel, and pour through the hold looting and slaying. King Kazador's own family is caught defenceless in his throne room, and many are hauled off into captivity in the dungeons of Black Crag. The king's son, Kazrik, is shaven and left behind, nailed in place onto his father's throne as a final insult to the old king. The Orcs leave the stronghold and make their escape, carrying much loot and many captives back to Black Crag.

2510   Battle of Broken Leg Gulley. After ten years of constant raiding and pillaging, the Orc Warlord Gnashrak is defeated by King Ungrim Ironfist of Karak Kadrin.

2519   Battle of a Hundred Cannons. A Goblin horde assails Zhufbar without warning but fails to breach the defences. An army from Karaz-a-Karak rapidly marches to the beleaguered hold's aid. The Goblins are quickly dispersed but it soon becomes evident that the Goblins have actually been fleeing a greater threat. Within weeks a powerful Ogre army bypasses Karak Kadrin and marches on the Moot. The armies of Karaz-a-Karak, Karak Kadrin and Zhufbar unite under High King Thorgrim Grudgebearer and give battle as the Ogres ford the River Aver. Just as the Ogres turn at bay, their forces divided by the river, an army of Men from Nuln arrives on the scene. Caught between the Dwarfs and Men, the Ogre ranks are swept by the largest concentration of artillery yet seen in the Old World and utterly destroyed.

2523   The Storm of Chaos erupts. Every pass through the Worlds Edge Mountains becomes a battlefield and every throng is mustered for war. Under the leadership of High King Thorgrim, the Dwarfs honour their alliances and defend their holds. While Orc tribes flock to Grimgor Ironhide's banner, High King Thorgrim commands King Alrik Ranulfsson to clear the Silver Road of Goblins and attack Mount Gunbad. Without the fighting power of the Orcs to oppose him, King Alrik settles many grudges with the Goblins and recovers many long-lost treasures.

THE DWARF REALMS

East of the Empire rise the ancient, snow-capped peaks of the Worlds Edge Mountains. Along their length, ridge after jagged ridge thrusts ever upward, marking the end of the civilised world. Extinct and still smoking volcanoes mark the great fault line that lies deep beneath the world's surface. The Dwarfs delve deep to find the rich veins of mineral wealth that occur in this area. As the Great Ice retreated from the world many thousands of years ago, grinding and shattering the rock into twisted peaks and deep chasms, the first Dwarf prospectors led their people northwards in search of riches. They discovered the wealth of the mountains, hewed their mines into the rock and founded their strongholds amid the loftiest peaks and the most inaccessible valleys.

The Dwarfs were not the only ones to make their homes in the mountains. As their settlements grew, they encountered other ancient races such as Orcs, Goblins, Giants, Trolls and Dragons. Both above the ground amidst the peaks and valleys, and in the dark beneath the world, the Dwarfs were forced to battle for their homes and treasures. Thus was forged the Dwarf race: determined, defiant, enterprising and brave, and so began the constant struggle for survival that the Dwarfs fight even to this day.

KARAZ~A~KARAK

The Dwarf language is complex and cannot be literally translated into the tongues of Men. Karaz-a-Karak can be roughly interpreted as 'Pinnacle of Mountains'. The Dwarf word for mountain also means 'a thing which endures', so an alternative translation is 'The Most Enduring'. Men call this city Everpeak, which is a good compromise in meaning. This mighty and populous stronghold was the ancient capital of the old Dwarf empire and its lord is the High King of all the Dwarfs. The noble clans of Karaz-a-Karak can trace a direct line of ancestry back to the Dwarf gods themselves. Here are the temples of the venerated Ancestor Gods: Grungni, Grimnir and Valaya. Here is kept the Great Book of Grudges and the Book of Remembering that are objects of awe and veneration in their own right.

Karaz-a-Karak has never fallen to an invader. It is the biggest, oldest and most fortified Dwarf stronghold. Here, the traditions of the old Dwarf empire are kept alive in their purest form. It is a city of ritual, temples, statues hewn from the rock and tombs in deep vaults below the city. The High King holds court in a vast vault large enough to engulf a small Human town. The forest of pillars which forms the mile-long nave is of truly colossal proportions. The whole vastness is illuminated by shafts of light, glowgems and great braziers so that the glint of gold, the gleam of bronze and the warm glow of the rock is everywhere. The tumult of the great throng assembled before the throne in council or in feasting is so raucous that it echoes in the vaults. Karaz-a-Karak has endured through ages past and will endure forever.

KARAK HIRN

Perched high above the world in the Black Mountains can be found Dwarf mines and trading outposts, small holds and valley settlements. These regions were settled slowly, and only grew in relative importance after the fall of the old Dwarf empire. They are not linked to the Underway, but are approached by treacherous mountain passes and cliff-hanging tracks. Rich deposits of precious metals and iron are found here, but there are fewer lodes of the more rare metals and gems. None of these settlements have become wealthy or powerful enough to rival the great strongholds of the Worlds Edge Mountains. However, they are closer and more accessible to the markets of the Empire and Tilea and act as trading centres for Dwarf work brought from further east.

The chief of these holds is Karak Hirn or Hornhold, so called because the winds blowing through an especially large cavern act like a mighty warhorn, sounding a frightening blast throughout the mountains. The Dwarfs have exploited this natural phenomenon by constructing additional sounding chambers, and massive doors that they can open and close to change the pitch and duration of the sound. By lighting fire in the depths, they can draw air through the system to create noise when they wish. The mountain horn is used to signal to outlying settlements, summon warriors and frighten away simple creatures such as Trolls.

KARAK AZUL

The name of this famed stronghold means 'Iron Peak' in the Dwarf language. The richest deposits of iron in all the Worlds Edge Mountains lie around Karak Azul. Other metals occur here too as well as gems in great quantity. The stronghold has become a centre of metalworking where some of the most skilled Dwarf weaponsmiths practice their art. Several of the stronghold's ancient clans claim direct descent from Grungni himself, the great Ancestor God.

Karak Azul is the last of the once great southern holds to remain under Dwarf control. Over the centuries, the other holds fell to the Goblins or were invaded by Skaven, but Karak Azul has endured, thanks in no small part to the determination and skill of its weaponsmiths. These days, Karak Azul supplies armaments to all the Dwarf holds and there are few weapons that can match the keenness of a blade made by its craftsmen. Many rune weapons are forged here where the secret art of runes is well understood. Weapons are carried out through hidden mountain trails and along the Underway to supply beleaguered outposts throughout the Worlds Edge Mountains.

KARAK KADRIN

Karak Kadrin means something like 'Stronghold of the Pass' in the Dwarf tongue. It stands south of the great Peak Pass, which in olden times enabled Dwarfs to travel between the western and eastern sides of the mountains. The importance of the route declined when the Dwarfs abandoned the eastern edge of the Worlds Edge Mountains. Today the pass must be guarded carefully, for it is one of the main routes by which invading Orcs and Goblins move westward from their lairs in the east. The Dwarfs of Karak Kadrin guard the Peak Pass against intruders.

Karak Kadrin is the home of fierce Dwarf clans who have set themselves the task of keeping the pass open, and it has never fallen, despite being besieged on many occasions. Karak Kadrin remains a wealthy centre for trade with the outside world, standing as it does overlooking the eastern part of the Empire and Kislev.

In times past, the King of Karaz-a-Karak, a proud individual named Baragor, suffered a terrible loss which drove him to become a Slayer, one of the cult of dishonoured Dwarfs who seek out death by fighting large and powerful monsters. However, as king his responsibilities to his kin could not be put aside, and so he remained as Lord of Karak Kadrin and did not disappear into the wilderness to find death. He became the first Slayer King, and because he was unable to seek death personally, he encouraged other Slayers to come to Karak Kadrin. He built the Shrine of the Slayers and collected tales of famous Slayers, paying the most talented bards to compose epic songs to commemorate their deeds. Since that time his descendants have been known as the Slayer Kings, and all carry the burden of the unfulfilled vow made by their ancestor. The current Slayer King of this tough and enduring stronghold is King Ungrim Ironfist.

BARAK VARR

Barak Varr means 'sea gate' in Khazalid, the Dwarf tongue. It is unique in that it is the only Dwarf stronghold located on the coast, its tunnels and caverns carved into the towering sea cliffs of the northern Black Gulf. Caves carved back into the rock carry the waters of the Black Gulf deep under the cliffs. Here, in vast water-filled caverns, the Dwarfs harbour their fleet. Dwarfs don't much like the sea or water, and their ships reflect their unease. Unlike the graceful ships of other races, their craft are made from iron and constructed very much like fortresses. With little patience for vagaries of the wind or tide, the Dwarfs propel their ships with paddles driven by pounding steam boilers.

Barak Varr is the most cosmopolitan of the Dwarf cities. Traders from every realm intermingle in its harbours, bringing goods from as far away as Araby and Cathay. The goods are carried up Skull River by the Dwarf ships, and then up through the Old Dwarf Road to Karaz-a-Karak and beyond. The Border Princes benefit greatly from the Dwarf domination of Blood River Valley, which would otherwise have been the front line against the Orc onslaughts.

KARAK IZOR

The Vaults consist of deep ice-cut valleys and towering heights and form the junction between the Black Mountains and the Grey Mountains. There are rich lodes of iron, copper, tin and other metals here and consequently some of the biggest and deepest mine workings outside the Worlds Edge Mountains. Many clans came here after the fall of their strongholds in the east, including many of the Dragonback Dwarfs. The valleys offered them seclusion from the outside world where they could work, remember the past and plan their ultimate return. The valleys and chasms are so difficult to reach that few evil creatures bother the Dwarfs of these highland areas. The most important stronghold in this area is Karak Izor, which is known to Men as Copper Mountain.

KARAK NORN

Although there are scattered communities of Dwarfs living under the Grey Mountains, they have never been very numerous or wealthy. The Grey Mountains are not blessed with the mineral deposits that especially attract Dwarfs and what little ore there is, is hard to mine. As a result, the Grey Dwarfs, as the inhabitants of this region are called, tend to be poor and rather simple in their tastes. Young Grey Dwarfs are likely to leave their lands and travel east in search of riches, and many become fierce prospectors and adventurers. The largest stronghold is Karak Norn that lies in the mountains above the Loren Forest.

THE WILD MOUNTAINS

The Dwarf strongholds are enclaves of order amongst the barren wilderness of the mountains. There are still many Dwarf settlements that lie outside the main strongholds, but these are small outposts and fortresses which pale into insignificance beside places like Karaz-a-Karak. Some of the most important mountain areas are described below:

BLACK FIRE PASS

This pass is called Haz-Drazh-Kadrin by the Dwarfs, but is more widely known as Black Fire Pass. It takes the form of a deep chasm through the Black Mountains, formed when volcanic eruptions rent apart the mountains in the distant past. Now the chasm is an eerie cleft of twisted lava and high black cliffs of polished volcanic glass. Strange black vapour blows from vents at the base of the cliffs. The pass is a favourite route through the mountains for invading Orc hordes and is also the principal route between the Empire and the sparsely settled lands of the Border Princes. An ancient Dwarf road leads through the pass on its way to Karaz-a-Karak.

MAD DOG PASS

The Dwarfs call this pass through the Worlds Edge Mountains Varag Kadrin. It is a common route through the mountains for tribes of Orc and Goblin raiders from the eastern side of the Worlds Edge Mountains and the Dark Lands beyond. In the days of the Dwarfs' greatest power, this was the chief thoroughfare to the eastern side of the mountains and the isolated mines of the Dark Lands. Today, the Dwarfs use the pass only occasionally, for it is studded with the fortresses of Night Goblins and its steep sides are riddled with their tunnels.

VOLCANOES

During the fall of the Dwarf empire, the Worlds Edge Mountains were shattered by earthquakes and riven by volcanoes. Huge cracks opened up and whole settlements were swallowed into the bowels of the earth. Boiling steam and molten rock poured through the lower galleries of many Dwarf strongholds, slaying thousands and sealing up areas forever. Since that time, the mountains have become quiet, but there are still a few volcanoes that sometimes erupt and cause havoc in the lands about.

The southern part of the Worlds Edge Mountains is far more temperamental than the north. There are three large volcanoes, although there are many smaller ones. The whole area is subject to minor earth tremors, and the Dwarfs often find their mines damaged or destroyed as a result. The three large volcanoes are called Karag Haraz, Karag Dron, and Karag Orrud. Amongst Men these are known as Fire Mountain, Thunder Mountain, and Red Cloud Mountain.

Volcanic activity in this region continually throws up new riches from the depths of the world. Enterprising Dwarf prospectors and miners come here to seek and extract the treasures of the earth, but mines and mining settlements are frequently destroyed by volcanic explosions or buried beneath ash or lava. Even in the face of this danger, the lure of wealth draws a constant stream of young Dwarfs from the faraway strongholds of the north.

ZHUFBAR

Zhufbar stands in a deep chasm down the mountainside from Black Water, a day's trek from Karak Varn. High above the city, a huge waterfall cascades from the lake and rushes fiercely down the chasm. Here the ingenious Dwarfs have constructed thousands of water wheels to power their drop hammers, ore crushers and washing pans. The chasm resounds to the noise of mining operations, creaking wheels and the rushing waters. The city contains the principle shrine of the Dwarf Engineers Guild and it is a centre for metalwork and every kind of industry. At night, the chasm glows with a thousand furnace fires. The meteoric iron gromril, mined in Karak Varn, used to be smelted here.

Zhufbar is surrounded by hostile Orc and Goblin tribes, while below ground the tunnels of the Skaven break into the Dwarf mines. Zhufbar has been attacked many times but has always managed to hold out. The deepest levels are dangerous places where Dwarfs and Skaven vie for control of the lower chambers.

BLACK WATER

In the Dwarf language, this vast lake is known as Varn Drazh, which means 'Black Water', and this is the name by which it is known to Men. The lake is formed from a vast crater filled with the melt water of the surrounding mountains. In the ancient past, a meteor crashed from the sky to pound this huge gaping crater out of the rock. All around the shores are to be found valuable metal ores, including the much-prized meteoric iron known as gromril, from which the hardest blades and armour are forged. Strongholds were founded around Varn Drazh to mine the meteoric metals, and also to harness the mountain torrents that gush from the lake. These raging waters wash the ore extracted from the mines and drive huge water wheels which in turn power the drop-hammers in the great subterranean forges. The lake itself is black and deep, and inhabited by dark and ancient monsters.

THE UNDERWAY

In the great days of the Dwarf empire, all the largest strongholds were linked by underground roads hacked through the solid rock. This complex system of tunnels is called the Underway or Ungdrin. From the main tunnel, other smaller tunnels led off to individual mines, forts, watchtowers and outlying strongholds. Nowadays, the system lies in ruins. It was partly destroyed by the massive eruptions that brought the Dwarf empire to its knees. This led the way to the tunnels being invaded by Skaven and Goblins, and many of the subsidiary branches were lost to these or other creatures. Over the years, other parts of the tunnels have collapsed or become dangerous.

Today the Ungdrin is unsafe. Not only is it prone to rockfalls, but also its length is often broken by chasms and pits that open up unexpectedly. Monsters of all kinds lurk in even the broadest and most structurally sound sections, and there are many Night Goblins living amongst the tunnels.

In recent years, routes through to the still-inhabited strongholds and outposts have been cleared and partially repaired. Although still dangerous, the Dwarfs are able to travel through the tunnels once more, although they only do so in large numbers and fully armed. Dwarf expeditions are frequently dispatched to explore and clear further sections of the old system. This is a continual battle, and one that faces constant setbacks and defeats. Nonetheless, the Dwarfs are gradually opening up some of their ancient mines and rediscovering the abandoned treasures of their ancestors.

DWARF SOCIETY

Each Dwarf hold is a self-contained economy. Most are at the centre of a network of smaller, subordinate holds that operate their own mines, farms and workshops. A vigorous trade exists between these holds and the great hold to which they owe allegiance. A more controlled trade goes on with other holds and with the outside world in general. The Empire, Tilea, Estalia and Bretonnia are all eager customers for Dwarf goods and Tilean merchants frequently act as middle-men ensuring that some exchange still goes on between Elves and Dwarfs despite both sides' antipathy towards each other.

The demand for Dwarf trade goods will never be sated. The Dwarfs are the finest artisans in the world and craft goods that are both elegant and robustly functional. The Dwarfs do not simply mass-produce, however. No true Dwarf could ever tolerate doing anything but his best work. Consequently, the supply of trade goods is kept relatively low, which has the fortunate effect of keeping the prices high.

There is little that the Dwarfs actually want for, partially because they maintain a stubborn disdain for other races' produce, and partially because, with the odd exception, Dwarfs have little use for fripperies and luxuries. The Dwarf population is relatively small and it is easy enough for them to provide for themselves by farming upland meadows, terraced fields within the boundary of the holds, fishing both surface and subterranean rivers and herding hardy mountain goats. This fare, while adequate, is less than exciting, so is augmented by trade. Particular attention is paid to different strains of hops and barley as the Dwarf palate demands a wide variety of ales and the brewer's craft is highly regarded.

As the proceeds of their industry are considerable and their expenses relatively slight, Dwarfs are able to indulge their natural tendency towards hoarding. They are also aggressive hagglers who will always seek to get the best side of a deal. Whilst this gives the Dwarf realm immense reserves of gold and gems, their reluctance to spend any of it diminishes its strategic value. Moreover, it helps to explain why Orcs and Goblins are willing to risk so much when attacking Dwarf holds. Even allowing for the fact that the choicest treasures will be cunningly concealed in vaults protected by traps of the greatest ingenuity, the loot that can be gained from a fallen hold is a prize unparalleled. It is no wonder that Orc Bosses spend the lives of their followers so generously in pursuit of such a prize.

SOCIAL STRUCTURE

Dwarf holds seem at first sight to have a social structure similar to human society. This is not surprising given that the Dwarfs helped inspire and shape the fledgling Empire. However, the distinctions between the social classes are based as much on honour and skill as they are on pure wealth, creating some subtle differences.

At the bottom of Dwarf society are clans that have been disgraced in some way. These are not allowed to join a guild and are often outcast from a hold. They may live in human lands or in their own settlements on the periphery of the Dwarf realm. These clans are looked down upon by other Dwarfs and many have, for centuries, been attempting to restore their reputation.

Above them are Dwarfs that have no home hold but whose clan's honour has not been besmirched in any way. All Dwarfs should have a hold and those that wander are regarded as being unconventional and therefore unreliable. Dwarfs from such clans are frequently traders, working in the cities of the Empire or travelling from hold to hold as necessity demands.

Next highest in the social order are Dwarfs who belong to respectable clans and dwell within established holds. They may be members of the less prestigious local guilds or may earn a living as labourers such as hrunki or skrundi. This category of Dwarf has little direct influence in hold affairs but has the respect of their peers.

At the top of the social order within any hold are clans who are members of the most respected trades such as goldsmiths, weaponsmiths, engineers and runesmiths. These clans are almost always associated with the great guilds, membership of which is often limited to members of those clans that originally formed the guild centuries ago.

The only higher ranked individuals in a hold will be the members of the royal clan. Dwarfs put great store in the lineage of their kings. Only if a royal line is extinguished (or, very rarely, disgraced) will it be changed. In such an event, there are several possibilities. A thane or prince from another hold may be invited to become king or another high-ranking clan may become the royal clan. Exactly what happens is decided in council by the thanes of the hold, with considerable wrangling from the guilds and the most influential clans.

Dwarfs are not fond of titles and like to keep such things simple. Apart from the king, and his direct

heirs, the princes, nobles are referred to as thanes, even if related to royalty. Thanes may hold offices, but these are not hereditary. Each swears an oath of allegiance to the king and holds his office at the king's whim.

When the call comes to muster, clans will form Warrior, Quarreller and Thunderer regiments under their own leader. The more affluent the clan, the more embellished their wargear will be. All Dwarf weaponry and armour is of excellent quality and even a minor clan will only send warriors to war properly harnessed.

GUILDS

Many long-established professions have guilds. A clan that practices a given profession will probably be affiliated to the guild. Some guilds ensure that only the clans that formed the guild are allowed to practice that trade (the practice is known as baren umbari – literally barring trade) to deny latecomers access to an established enterprise.

Guilds set out rules for member clans to follow. Dwarfs attach considerable importance to having a recognised trade or craft so are normally willing to obey guild rules.

Within each guild, Dwarfs follow the standard path of apprentice, journeyman and master. A council, comprising all the guild's masters, is responsible for enforcing the rules and regulating the guild. Expulsion from a guild is a serious dishonour. Failure to exile an expelled guild member from a clan can bring the same punishment down on the clan.

In wartime, it is customary for members of clan regiments to display guild insignia on their banners and shields; this is not a uniform, merely a reflection of the pride that individual warriors take in their guild.

THE GUILD OF ENGINEERS

The most powerful guild is the Guild of Engineers, which many claim was founded by Grungni. The guild attempts to regulate the most inventive of Dwarfs, ensuring that everything they make is based on proven, reliable engineering principles. This is sadly a losing battle as Dwarf Engineers are constantly striving for the invention that will carry their name forever. This makes relations between the guild and its most illustrious guild members more than a little strained. Virtually every Engineer visionary has at some point been expelled from the guild, only to be readmitted later when their invention finally wins acceptance. This may, of course, be long after their deaths. In the meantime, exile and derision is the anvil on which many a true Engineer is shaped.

KHAZALID

The ancient high language of the Dwarfs is called Khazalid. It is a deeply conservative language that has not changed noticeably in many thousands of years either in its spoken or written 'runic' form. The Dwarfs are very proud of their tongue which they rarely speak in the company of other races and never teach to other creatures. To humans it is the 'secret tongue of the Dwarfs', occasionally overheard, but never properly understood.

The sound of Khazalid is not much like human speech and very unlike the melodious sound of Elvish. Comparisons have been drawn to the rumble of thunder. All Dwarfs have very deep, resonant voices and a tendency to speak more loudly than is strictly necessary. This can make Dwarfs sound rowdy and irascible – which for the most part is a fair reflection of Dwarvish temperament. The vocabulary of Khazalid ably reflects the unique preoccupations of the Dwarf race. There are hundreds of words for different kinds of rock, for

passages and tunnels, and most of all for precious metals. Indeed, there are hundreds of words for gold alone, reflecting on its qualities of colour, lustre, purity and hardness. In their dealings with others, Dwarfs choose their words carefully. A Dwarf will not venture an opinion on anything that he has not considered deeply, and once his mind is made up you can be sure his view will be as immovable as a mountain. Dwarfs don't change their opinions except in the face of overwhelming necessity – and not always then. Many would rather die stubbornly than admit to a mistake that costs them their life! For this reason, Dwarfs take oaths and promises very seriously indeed. In all the Dwarf language, the word 'unbaraki' is the most condemning of all – it means 'oathbreaker'.

Curiously the Dwarf word for the race of Men is 'umgi' whilst its abstract form of 'umgak' means 'shoddy' – the Dwarf word being equivalent to 'man-made'.

THE DWARF THRONG

SPECIAL RULES

The following special rules apply to all the models in a Dwarf army.

Ancestral Grudge. Dwarfs hold grudges for a long time, possibly forever. They have never forgiven the fall of their strongholds at the hands of the Orcish enemy. Dwarfs *hate* all types of Orcs, Goblins and Snotlings, including Night Goblins, Black Orcs, Hobgoblins, Gnoblars... in fact all Greenskins of any description!

Resolute. Dwarfs fight with grim determination and are reluctant to abandon their position. Dwarfs (but not Gyrocopters) flee and pursue 2D6-1" instead of the normal 2D6".

Relentless. A Dwarf on the march is as implacable as the turning of the years, and just as impossible to halt. Dwarf units may march even if there are enemy close enough to inhibit march moves.

EQUIPMENT

Dwarf Handgun

The handguns of Dwarf Thunderers, called 'dragon belchers' by the more superstitious Goblin tribes, feature many improvements over the crude devices used by other races. These features include rifled barrels, finer powder grain and more reliable firing mechanisms.

Maximum Range: 24"; **Strength:** 4

Rules: Armour piercing; Move-or-fire.

Superior design: A Dwarf handgun has a +1 to hit modifier.

Gromril Armour

Armour made from the metal known as gromril is the toughest and sturdiest in the known world. Known variously as meteoric iron, silverstone and hammernought armour, gromril armour is limited to wealthy Dwarfs and the elite Ironbreakers.

Rules: Gromril armour gives a 4+ Armour Save.

Oath Stones

When a Dwarf goes to war he carries the honour of his clan and his hold with him. It is a matter of personal pride that he will do them credit or not return at all. To demonstrate his intent he will take an Oath stone with him. This is a carefully sculpted plinth on which the lineage and the deeds of the owner are carved.

At the start of the game, a character with an Oath stone must nominate a unit of Warriors (but NOT Rangers), Longbeards, Ironbreakers or Hammerers to be his Stonebearers. The character must deploy with this unit and cannot leave it during the game. The presence of the stone with the unit confers Magic Resistance (1) as its runes act to absorb wild magic. No other character may join a Stonebearer unit.

Furthermore, while the character lives, if the Stonebearer unit is charged, the character may 'set the stone' and stand upon it as part of a Hold reaction. This indicates that he has chosen to stand and fight where he is. Accordingly his Stonebearers, inspired by his resolve, form up around him, facing in all directions. It is not necessary to move the models to represent this.

Setting the stone has the following effects:

1) The Stonebearer unit has no flanks or rear from this point, even if the character on the stone is killed. This means, for example, that they do not lose their rank bonuses if charged in flank or rear, that no enemy unit gets a combat resolution bonus for attacking them in flank or rear and so on.

2) The Stonebearer unit may not move in any way unless forced to Flee and may not choose to Flee as a charge reaction. The character on the stone may not be moved within the unit.

3) A Character on an Oath stone must always issue a challenge in close combat and meet any challenge whether he is fighting or not (he is not hard to find – he's the one on the stone!).

4) If the Stonebearer unit flees, then the Oath stone is lost. Also the Victory Points for the owning character are lost whether he survives the battle or not, such is his dishonour.

LORDS & THANES

The most powerful fighters in a Dwarf army are its Lords and Thanes. Each of them has vast experience combating the enemies of their race, often built up over several centuries. Dwarf leaders are well tutored in the art of war, learning both from the elders of their own clans and the venerable Runesmiths. When the time comes for them to lead, they will have learnt more than most commanders ever know and will have been tried and tested on the battlefield many times. This experience and wisdom is reflected in their beards, a clear indication that the other Dwarfs in the throng would do well to follow their example.

When battle is joined it is the Lords & Thanes, with their finely crafted armour and rune-inscribed axes who seek out the enemy's most powerful combatants, matching bestial fury or dark magic with courage, honour and honest steel.

	M	WS	BS	S	T	W	I	A	Ld
Lord	3	7	4	4	5	3	4	4	10
Thane	3	6	4	4	5	2	3	3	9

SHIELDBEARERS

A Dwarf General may be carried into battle atop a shield carried by two loyal (and strong) retainers.

A General and his Shieldbearers fight as a single model with a Unit Strength of 3 (even in challenges). They are mounted on a 40mm wide by 20mm deep base. The Shieldbearers add 2 to the Armour Save of the character (to a maximum of 1+) mounted on the shield. The Shieldbearers give the General two extra WS5 Strength 4 Initiative 3 close combat attacks each round but these attacks do not benefit from any weapon (runic or otherwise) carried by the General.

If a General with Shieldbearers fights with a unit, he counts as two normal models for the purposes of working out if there is a complete rank of four models. Note that when in a unit, a Lord and his Shieldbearers may still use the 'Look out, Sir!' rule and are not considered a larger target than the other unit members.

ROYAL BLOOD

Dwarf Lords (but Thanes) are of Royal Blood. This special rule is used in conjunction with the Bodyguard special rule – refer to the Hammerer entry for details.

In addition, if an army contains a character with Royal Blood, it may have one more unit of Longbeards than it does Warriors. These represent the Dwarfs of the character's own clan.

DWARF KINGS

Each of the major holds (known as Karaks) has its own king. The title of king is a hereditary one within the ruling clan. The title passes from the king to his eldest son upon the king's death. Sometimes, when a king does not have an heir, or his heir is unsuited to rule, another heir must be selected. In this case one of the king's duties is to select and supervise the training of his successor from within his clan. Naturally enough such important decisions are made in conjunction with the Council of Elders. The council is made up of the oldest and wisest Dwarfs in the hold and commands respect accordingly. A king will rarely act against the direct advice of his council although by the same token a council will rarely question the wisdom of a king who has proven his mettle. This makes for a very stable government indeed.

At any time there will be a single High King. Since the time of Gotrek Starbreaker this has normally been the King of Karaz-a-Karak. This is a reflection of its status as the most powerful hold, certainly since the fall of Karak Eight Peaks. The High King nominally commands the allegiance of all the other kings, however, in practice, this is normally a matter of cooperation rather than command as Dwarfs, and particularly Dwarf kings, are proud individuals not accustomed to blind obedience.

There have been examples of Dwarf queens. This has been limited to small holds in the past. In most cases a queen is not a long-term ruler but merely a short-term figurehead until a suitable husband can be found for her. Naturally enough a queen is a fine catch for the right Dwarf so their independent reigns tend to be very brief.

RUNESMITHS

The ancient Guild of Runesmiths is one of the oldest and most respected institutions in all the Dwarf realms. According to tradition, its origins stretch back to the days of Grungni, the great Ancestor God of Mining, Master of the Forge and Lord of the Runes. The Runesmiths Guild claims descent from Grungni's son Morgrim. For this reason, the Runesmiths sometimes refer to themselves as the Clan of Morgrim, although they are not the only clan to claim descent from Grungni or his sons. All Runesmiths are related to each other in some, often very remote, fashion. Each carries on his family's traditions of arcane study, learning the ancient craftsmanship of working metal and magic into mighty runes of power. Although some other races make magic items of great potency, Runesmiths are masters of the art. The greatest Runesmiths are superlative craftsmen, widely respected by all Dwarfs, and even accorded the sort of reverence normally reserved for ancestors.

The number of Runesmiths is not very great. When a Runesmith judges that it is time, he chooses a young relative as his apprentice and teaches him the secrets of making magic runes. Runesmiths are very secretive about their knowledge and will only pass it on to a worthy successor. Many powerful runes have been lost simply because a Runesmith could find no one worthy enough to succeed him. However, Runesmiths do tend to live for a long time even by Dwarf standards. As Dwarfs get older they get tougher, even more obstinate, and extremely stubborn. These great heroes and lords can proudly sit at the tables of kings, and their immense age accords a status not possible amongst Men or Elves.

Runesmiths are ancient and powerful individuals. At the very least they will have endured hundreds of years of harsh apprenticeship under the demanding eye and unforgiving hand of their forebear. Older Runesmiths will have survived hundreds of years of further toil, centuries of beating runes from hot metal, and decades of searching out old secrets in the depths of lost Dwarf strongholds. As a result, it is hard to imagine a tougher or more cantankerous Dwarf.

	M	WS	BS	S	T	W	I	A	Ld
Runesmith	3	5	4	4	4	2	2	2	9
Runelord	3	6	4	4	5	3	3	2	9

Rune Lore

A Runesmith gives the Dwarf player an extra Dispel dice in the enemy Magic phase. A Runelord gives the Dwarf player an extra two Dispel dice in the enemy Magic phase.

ANVIL OF DOOM

The Anvils of Doom are the most ancient heirlooms of the Dwarf race. It is on these anvils that the greatest rune weapons have been forged. Each anvil is covered in runes that modern Runesmiths cannot begin to fathom. When striking runes on the anvil, each Runelord uses techniques taught to him by his master that were in turn taught to him by his master and so on back to the dawn of time. Because of this, no two anvils function in exactly the same way. Their powers can be broken down into three broad categories: those dedicated to Grimnir that emphasise fury, those dedicated to Grungni that emphasise effort and those dedicated to Valaya that emphasise loyalty.

A Dwarf army may have one and only one Anvil of Doom. In gaming terms, the Anvil is a war machine that cannot be moved and cannot be attacked at all, by any means (no more than you can move or attack a hill!).

Whenever a Runelord brings an Anvil of Doom to the battlefield, two Anvil Guards always accompany him. The Guards have sworn the most binding oaths never to abandon the Anvil or the Runelord to the enemy. Each Anvil Guard fights using the profile below.

	M	WS	BS	S	T	W	I	A	Ld
Anvil Guard	3	5	3	4	4	1	2	1	9

The Runelord and the two Anvil Guards must remain for all the battle on the platform. They are Unbreakable, may not declare charges and will never pursue beaten foes. The Anvil and crew have a Unit Strength of 5. No other characters may join the Anvil crew.

Enemy units that charge the Anvil model are placed in base contact with the platform. The Runelord and the Guards place themselves between the enemy and the Anvil, without leaving the Anvil's platform. The Anvil and crew count as a unit with a 60mm wide frontage for the purposes of close combat.

When shooting at the Anvil of Doom, randomise hits evenly between the remaining Dwarfs. To take into account the protection offered by the Anvil, the Runelord and Anvil Guards gain a 4+ Ward Save against any form of missile (this includes magic missiles as well as normal missiles).

Equipment
The Anvil Guard wear gromril armour and each carries a hand weapon and shield.

Victory Points
- Score Victory Points for the Runelord as normal.

- If the Runelord and both guards are killed then Victory Points are scored for the Runelord as normal and the Anvil in addition.

Dispel Dice
While the owning Runelord lives, an Anvil adds an extra dice to the Dwarfs' Dispel pool.

STRIKING RUNES ON THE ANVIL OF DOOM

During his own Shooting phase the Runelord may strike a single rune each turn. A rune may not be struck if the Runesmith or Guards are in close combat. Anvils are ancient beyond reckoning and have powers that few Runesmiths dare to call upon. When striking a rune, a Runesmith must choose whether he will strike it normally or try to call forth its ancient power.

A rune is struck correctly on a D6 roll of 2+ if struck normally, 4+ if struck with ancient power. If the rune is not struck correctly, roll a D6 and consult the Failed Rune table to determine the effect on the Anvil.

FAILED RUNE TABLE

D6 Result

1 Disaster! The Runelord makes a critical error and the Anvil is split in two by the discharge of energy. Remove the Anvil, the Runelord and the Anvil Guards as casualties immediately.

2-3 In striking the rune, the Runelord draws more power from the Anvil than he can control. The rune does not take effect and the Anvil may not be used to strike runes in the following turn.

4-6 The rune is struck incorrectly, the magical energies are dissipated into the earth and no effect is produced this turn.

RUNE OF HEARTH & HOLD

The Rune of Hearth and Hold was originally the gift of Valaya to the Dwarfs. With each blow of the hammer a low bass note resonates across the battlefield, reminding all friendly Dwarf units of hold, clan and ancestors. Every friendly Dwarf unit may re-roll failed Fear or Terror tests while the note lasts. Remember you may never re-roll a re-roll.

The note lasts until the start of the owning player's next Shooting phase.

Ancient Power. If the Runelord attempts to use the full power of the runes then all friendly Dwarf units may re-roll failed Panic and Break tests, and are immune to *fear* and *terror* while the note lasts.

RUNE OF OATH & HONOUR

When the runes are struck, Grungni's blessing is placed upon the works of the Dwarfs. The Dwarfs, whose resolution and endurance is legend anyway, are driven to make an extra supernatural effort to ensure that they do their duty. A single, friendly Dwarf unit (but not a Gyrocopter) may make a normal move (which can be a March or Charge) in the Shooting phase.

Units that move in this way may not shoot in the Shooting phase. Units which rallied earlier in the turn may not make this move.

Ancient Power. If the Runelord uses the full power of the runes then D3 friendly Dwarf units will be affected.

RUNE OF WRATH & RUIN

When the Anvil is struck and the name of Grimnir is invoked, the power of the Rune of Wrath & Ruin causes the sky to darken and the earth to crack, venting fire and sulphur. Nominate an unengaged enemy unit anywhere on the table. You may not target independent characters unless they (or their mounts) are large targets. The target unit takes D6 magical Strength 4 hits distributed in the same way as Shooting hits. If that unit has the Fly ability then it cannot Fly in its next Movement phase. If it is not a Flyer then its Movement characteristic is halved until the end of its own following turn. If forced to flee, for whatever reason, the unit flees at half speed (determine the flee distance of the unit as normal and then halve the score, rounding up).

Ancient Power. If the Runelord attempts to use the full power of the runes then D3 enemy units are affected and each takes 2D6 magical Strength 4 hits.

WARRIORS

Dwarfs are immensely strong and resilient, broad of shoulder, wide in the girth, with big hands and broad feet. They are ideally adapted to cope with demanding physical work, and can dig or tunnel for hours without tiring. Their extreme physical endurance also enables them to carry heavy loads without any notable loss in speed. As well as being physically robust they are also mentally tough. To say that a Dwarf knows his own mind is something of an understatement.

Dwarfs are set in their ways and extremely determined. They are supremely confident in the virtues and values of their civilisation, and are openly scornful of the achievements of other 'less accomplished' races. This combination of physical and mental durability makes Dwarfs steadfast fighters. They will often fight to the last rather than admit defeat, and rarely run away even if the situation appears hopeless.

Dwarfs take matters of oaths and bargains very seriously indeed. A Dwarf who is unable for some reason to keep a bargain he has made will suffer considerable anguish and loss of face. Often, the shame will prove too much to bear, and he will abandon his family to wander in the mountains, or even become a Slayer.

Although very determined and matter-of-fact in their daily lives, once a Dwarf snaps his whole life collapses like a mighty tree blown down in the wind. It is because they take such matters so seriously that they rarely forgive acts of betrayal or disloyalty. In fact, if there's one thing a Dwarf can do better than anything else it is hold a grudge! The Dwarfs have never forgiven the High Elves for starting the ancient war between their two races. Even though Dwarfs and Elves now enjoy comparatively friendly relations, it is unlikely that the Dwarfs will ever trust them completely again.

	M	WS	BS	S	T	W	I	A	Ld
Warrior	3	4	3	3	4	1	2	1	9
Veteran	3	4	3	3	4	1	2	2	9

LONGBEARDS

Longbeards are the oldest, most experienced Dwarf warriors, a fact evidenced by the length of their beards. These ensure that they receive complete respect from other Dwarfs, who have been taught quite rightly to respect their elders.

Longbeards have fought in more wars, beaten more enemies, and endured greater hardships than any young Dwarf can imagine. They constantly grumble about how today's Goblins are far smaller and weedier than they used to be and how nothing is as well made as it was in their day. No Dwarf would gainsay them as they have the experience and the beard to prove it.

In battle, Longbeards are able to demonstrate their time-won skills, disdainful of any minor shifts in fortune that would throw less experienced warriors into confusion, and woe betide any beardling who falters under their stern eye, for they will admonish him in no uncertain terms.

	M	WS	BS	S	T	W	I	A	Ld
Longbeard	3	5	3	4	4	1	2	1	9
Veteran	3	5	3	4	4	1	2	2	9

Immune to Panic. Longbeards expect the worst, and spend a long time grumbling about the inadequacies of Dwarfs/weapons/Goblins these days, as they're not as brave/well made/scary as they were in the olden days. It takes a lot to unsettle a Longbeard from a good grumble. Longbeards automatically pass any Panic tests they have to take.

Old Grumblers. Longbeards tend to look down their beards at younger Dwarfs. In their turn other Dwarfs pay dutiful attention to the words of their elders. Any Dwarf unit within 6" of a unit of non-fleeing Longbeards may re-roll failed Panic tests to avoid their withering glares and endless moans of "told you so!".

SLAYERS

Dwarfs are above all very proud individuals and do not cope easily with failure or personal loss. Should a Dwarf suffer some terrible personal tragedy, he will be inconsolable. The loss of his family, his hoard, or failure to uphold a promise can seriously unhinge the mind of any Dwarf. Young Dwarfs forsaken in love often never recover from the blow to their pride. Whatever the cause, Dwarfs who have suffered what they perceive to be a serious loss of honour will often forsake the fellowship of their family and friends for a life of self-imposed exile.

Leaving their home stronghold as far behind as possible, they wander in the wilderness brooding on the misery of existence. Having broken with everything he holds dear, the Dwarf deliberately seeks death by hunting out and fighting large monsters. These Dwarfs are called Slayers. They are stern and laconic individuals, not much given to talking about themselves, and they tend to be horribly scarred as a result of their encounters with Trolls, Giants, Dragons and other monsters.

Slayers dye their hair bright orange, and stiffen it with pig grease so that it sticks out at alarming angles. Their way of life invariably means that many achieve their ambition and are slain at the hands of whatever ferocious beast they have confronted. Others, the least successful ones in a sense, tend to survive either because they are the toughest, the fastest or most determined. This process of natural selection weeds out all those who do not have exceptional abilities, so you can be fairly sure that any Slayer you meet is exceptionally tough, violent, and psychopathically dangerous.

Slayers are a fascinating sub-cult of Dwarf society, and many famous Slayers have achieved deeds of exceptional valour. Younger Slayers often band together, sometimes under the tutelage of an older master, so that they can learn the arts of monster slaying. Slayers spend as much time as possible improving their warrior skills. Although they seek death, Dwarfs are incapable of deliberately fighting to lose, and so always enter the fray to win.

	M	WS	BS	S	T	W	I	A	Ld
Troll Slayer	3	4	3	3	4	1	2	1	10
Giant Slayer	3	5	3	4	4	1	3	2	10
Dragon Slayer	3	6	3	4	5	2	4	3	10
Daemon Slayer	3	7	3	4	5	3	5	4	10

Unbreakable. Note, however, that Slayers still *hate* Greenskins.

Loner. Daemon Slayers and Dragon Slayers may only fight alone or join a Slayers unit. Daemon Slayers and Dragon Slayers can never be the army's General.

Slayer. All Slayers have an uncanny ability that makes them particularly effective against especially tough opponents. When rolling to wound, a Slayer's Strength, including any modifiers for weapons (eg, a great axe), is increased until it is equal to the Toughness of his opponent, up to a maximum of Strength 6. If the opponent's Toughness is lower than the Slayer's Strength, including any additional modifiers for weapons, the Slayer does not receive any Strength bonus. For example, a Slayer armed with a great axe (S5) is fighting a Dragon (T6): normally he needs a 5+ to wound, but because of the Slayer skill his Strength is increased to 6 and he therefore wounds on a 4+. Note that the Armour Save modifier is calculated at the modified Strength score, in this case it is -3 for a Strength 6 hit. If the Slayer were fighting a weedy Goblin (T3), he would use his normal Strength of 5 and would therefore wound the Goblin on a 2+, with an Armour Save modifier of -2.

Slayer Axes. Slayers are skilled with all manner of axes and carry a mixture of single- and double-handed axes around with them. At the start of any combat, a Slayer unit may choose to fight either with two axes counting as having an additional hand weapon, or to take a single axe in both hands, counting it as a great weapon. If the Slayer has a rune axe then this rule ceases to apply and he fights with the rune axe only, generally as a hand weapon but possibly as a great weapon if it has the Master Rune of Kragg the Grim inscribed on it.

Once they have made the choice on how to use their axes they must continue doing this until the combat is over.

QUARRELLERS

Since the Dwarfs first came to the Worlds Edge Mountains the crossbow has ever been their ranged weapon of choice. It will easily outrange the puny bows of the Goblins and is powerful enough to drop even a Black Orc in his tracks. In more recent times, devotees of the handgun have grown in numbers to the extent that the crossbow is no longer entirely the dominant weapon. The crossbow will never disappear entirely though. The Quarrellers that remain are a stubborn bunch, preferring to trust their own estimates of range and wind than rely on a new-fangled sight. If nothing else, many of them begrudge the cost of powder when a bit of elbow grease will propel a quarrel as far as a bullet.

	M	WS	BS	S	T	W	I	A	Ld
Quarreller	3	4	3	3	4	1	2	1	9
Veteran	3	4	3	3	4	1	2	2	9

THUNDERERS

Although some more traditional Dwarfs still regard the handgun with suspicion, it has become as common a sight in Dwarf armies as the crossbow. The Dwarfs who specialise in the handgun have become known as Thunderers. Being naturally methodical as well as mechanically gifted, they will continue to load and fire in a disciplined manner, even when the enemy are right on them, rarely suffering the misfires that would afflict less-disciplined troops. Many Thunderers will have crafted their own handguns, incorporating additional improvements of their own or the latest ideas from noted Engineers. There is some rivalry between Thunderers regarding what makes for the most accurate weapon, resulting in Dwarf handguns being the most precise weapons of their type in the world.

	M	WS	BS	S	T	W	I	A	Ld
Thunderer	3	4	3	3	4	1	2	1	9
Veteran	3	4	3	3	4	1	2	2	9

RANGERS

Not all Dwarfs live in great holds under the mountains. Some clans dwell above ground, trading with Men and operating their own businesses such as mines and breweries. For such clans the battle against the Greenskins is a daily challenge, with raiding commonplace. The tradition has developed for Dwarfs to band together to defend their communities against these threats and to settle grudges by hunting down the culprits. Such bands have become known as Rangers. Armed with their preferred great axes, bands of Rangers have brought a bloody reckoning to many an enemy of Dwarfkind.

HAMMERERS

Hammerers are the king's personal guard and so are accorded a high status within the stronghold. They are very skilled warriors and are personally selected by the king himself. If a Dwarf should prove himself courageous enough over the course of many battles he may be selected to join the Hammerers. Skill, strength and courage alone, however, are not enough. A Hammerer must be willing to give his complete loyalty to his liege and dedicate himself totally to protecting him from harm. Amongst a folk known throughout the world for their stubbornness, Hammerers are regarded as being stubborn by other Dwarfs.

Duty to king and hold is a sacred thing to Dwarfs. A Dwarf bound by oath to serve a king will give his life rather than face the dishonour of failure. A king surrounded by his Hammerers is the keep in the centre of the throng: grim-faced, unyielding and immovable, the living personification of the Dwarf spirit.

The symbol of the bond between a Lord and his Hammerers is the weapon they carry. Each bears a heavy, but perfectly balanced, great hammer. It is the gift of the hammer to the warrior that seals the oath between him and his Lord. In battle, the sight of the great hammers rising and falling around the King's banner is an inspiration to the rest of the throng who will typically redouble their own efforts to keep up.

	M	WS	BS	S	T	W	I	A	Ld
Hammerer	3	5	3	4	4	1	2	1	9
Gate Keeper	3	5	3	4	4	1	2	2	9

Stubborn. Hammerers are Stubborn as described in the Warhammer rulebook.

Bodyguard. Hammerers are selected from the steadiest and most resolute Dwarfs. If the unit is joined by a character with the Royal Blood special rule then the unit and the character become Immune to Fear and Terror.

MINERS

Dwarfs have an insatiable thirst for gold, and construct deep shafts beneath the mountains in their quest for more of it, but it is not the only thing that fuels their interest in mining. Gemstones and ores are also especially valued, many Dwarf crafts being dependent on a regular supply of both.

Dwarfs are ideally suited to be miners, their strength and endurance making them excellent wielders of pick, hammer and shovel. They also have an instinct for the stone, knowing where best to dig and when to pause to shore up a section of tunnel. Collapses and other accidents are rare. The longer established a mine is, the more mechanical contrivances there will be. Steam-powered engines, fixed in position, continually haul chains which tow wagons out of the depths. Some clans may even use a new-fangled boring machine that some Engineer has invented. But, however successful these are, they can never replace the skill and experience of a Dwarf Miner.

When a Dwarf hold goes to war, many mining clans will send their warriors to battle. As a gesture of pride in their profession, they will tend to carry picks rather than axes but such is their skill with them that this is no disadvantage. There are many benefits to having such troops in an army, notably they can use their skills to tunnel beneath the enemy and gain the advantage of surprise.

	M	WS	BS	S	T	W	I	A	Ld
Miner	3	4	3	3	4	1	2	1	9
Prospector	3	4	3	3	4	1	2	2	9

Underground Advance. Miners are famous for using their extensive knowledge of underground tunnels to make their way to the enemy's rear and turn up on the battlefield from a completely unexpected direction.

Miners do not have to be deployed on the table at the beginning of the battle.

Instead, starting from turn two, at the beginning of every Dwarf turn roll a dice: on a 4+ the Miners will arrive. For every successive turn after the second, add a further +1 to the roll, so they arrive on a 3+ in turn three, and so on (but an unmodified roll of 1 is always a failure).

In the Movement phase of the turn when they arrive, Miners can enter the battlefield from any table edge and will be treated exactly like a unit that has pursued an enemy off the table in the previous turn (see the Warhammer rulebook). If the Miners fail to turn up for the entire game, they have obviously got lost in the tunnels, but their points are not awarded to the opponent.

Steam Drill. The steam drill is a piece of mining equipment that is also of use on the battlefield. A small steam engine, usually alcohol-powered, is used to drive the hammer with such force that it can punch through rock with ease. A Dwarf Miner unit using Underground Advance that is equipped with a steam drill may re-roll its arrival dice each turn until it arrives. This represents the Miners taking a shortcut straight through the rock! It is also a nasty weapon in close combat, requiring two hands to use, striking last and conferring +3 Strength to its wielder.

Blasting Charges. Miners are extremely skilled in the art of using black powder to blast their way to mineral deposits. Needless to say something this destructive can be useful in a tight spot during battles and sieges.

Miners equipped with blasting charges may use them as a thrown weapon when making Stand & Shoot responses. One enemy unit charging the Miners will take D6 Flaming Strength 6 hits allocated as shooting. This attack has a nominal range of 4".

Blasting charges are one use only.

DEFENCE OF THE HOLD

Although the Dwarfs are a martial race, skilled in all the arts of war, there are few professional Dwarf soldiers. The majority of Dwarfs are craftsmen and artisans who, when called upon by their clan leader, will organise into regiments to fight for king and hold. Within each clan, the Longbeards form a core of professional warriors, and instruct the others, often while in a tavern. In return, they are released from their more mundane duties to practice their skills. Similarly, the hold's Hammerers form the king's permanent bodyguard and have special responsibilities for guarding the gates of the hold. Ironbreaker regiments are charged with guarding the underground approaches and, like the Hammerers, are perpetually under arms.

Because only a fraction of the available Warriors are on duty at any time, the Dwarfs depend on getting early warning of attacks. Around each hold is a network of fortifications ranging from squat bastions to observation posts on the high peaks, many connected by tunnels both to each other and the hold itself. As an enemy approaches they will find themselves under fire from war machines placed in the bastions, delaying and disrupting their advance. The legendary ingenuity of the Dwarfs is manifest in the variety and sophistication of the outer defences. Finally, the invader will be confronted with the readied defences of the hold itself, which are impervious to anything other than a long siege.

Depending on the circumstances, the king may choose to take the battle to the invaders, perhaps emerging with his mustered throng from hidden gates to strike by surprise. A quick victory is always preferable. The longer the throng is at war, the poorer the hold gets so it suits all concerned to settle things as quickly as is prudent to ensure that the mines and workshops can return to normal. Sometimes a half-throng or quarter-throng will be called. Here only a proportion of each clan's strength is mustered, allowing a longer campaign, knowing that the hold is secure and prosperous.

IRONBREAKERS

Most of Karaz Ankor lies beneath the ground. From the towering vaults and labyrinthine galleries of the holds to the endless tunnels of the Underway. Adjoining these are the shafts of countless mines and the dark, dangerous warrens of the Goblins and Skaven. This is a part of the Everlasting Realm that remains a mystery to all but the Dwarfs and their ancestral enemies.

All manner of fell creatures lurk below and the Ironbreakers guard the deep abandoned tunnels from those that would otherwise invade the hold. They spend much of their time below ground in the deepest, least visited parts of the stronghold. In these dark places, ambush and rockfall are commonplace hazards and survival is often dependent on wearing the right armour. Accordingly, Ironbreakers wear fine suits of gromril armour, crafted by the smiths of the hold and worn as a badge of honour by this select band of warriors.

Such is the reputation of the Ironbreakers that they will often be called upon to fight on the surface when the full might of a throng is mustered, but for each battle in sunlight, an Ironbreaker will have fought a dozen in the dark deeps beneath the mountains.

	M	WS	BS	S	T	W	I	A	Ld
Ironbreaker	3	5	3	4	4	1	2	1	9
Ironbeard	3	5	3	4	4	1	2	2	9

ENGINEERS GUILD

The Dwarf Engineers Guild is one of the most secretive of all Dwarf institutions and over the centuries its members have honed their skills of precision engineering to a fine art. Most of their inventions are practical and functional: pumps to clear water from mine workings, engines to draw cages up vertical shafts, and steam-powered hammers to beat out sheet metal. Ever since the guild's founding they have also developed machines for battle, initially the simple Bolt Thrower and Grudge Thrower but they soon mastered the art of cannon founding. Over time, individual Engineers, eager to make a name for themselves, have come up with even more deadly inventions to unleash upon the enemies of the Everlasting Realm.

There are many wild rumours about the way the Engineers Guild operates, many of them coming from former members of the guild. On the battlefield, however, an Engineer is able to offer vital advice on the positioning of artillery and its use. In addition, they are useful Dwarfs in a tight spot, often carrying the latest pistols and handguns.

MASTER ENGINEER

A Master Engineer is expert in many fields. He is first and foremost a doughty warrior whose skill alone merits a place of honour in the Dwarf throng. In addition, he is a consummate craftsman who can perform any task relating to metal or stone from forging cannon barrels to designing steam engines to drafting the plans for fortifications and mines.

A throng which utilises several war machines will often be accompanied by a Master Engineer. Not only can he help to repair damage done to these cherished machines but he can also direct their crews with a skill born of intimate familiarity with the workings of each device.

	M	WS	BS	S	T	W	I	A	Ld
Master Engineer	3	4	5	4	4	2	2	2	9

Artillery Master. The Master Engineer is adept at operating artillery.

• If he joins a Bolt Thrower, you may use his BS.

• If he joins a Grudge Thrower, you may re-roll the Artillery dice (but not the Scatter dice) when firing it.

• If he joins a Cannon, it inflicts D6 wounds on enemy hit rather than the normal D3.

Entrenchment. A Dwarf army contains many skilled workers that can be put to good use by a Master Engineer. Up to one war machine (not a Gyrocopter!) may be entrenched per Master Engineer in the army. An entrenched war machine is treated as being in hard cover when shot at, and as protected by a defended obstacle if attacked in close combat. An entrenched war machine can be pivoted to fire but if it moves in any other way, the entrenchment is lost. If the war machine is destroyed, the entrenchment is lost at the same time.

ENGINEER

Some Dwarf war machine crews may include an Engineer. Whilst not as accomplished as a Master Engineer, an Engineer confers some advantages to his war machine.

	M	WS	BS	S	T	W	I	A	Ld
Engineer		3	4	4	3	4	1	2	1	9

Artillery Specialist. Some Dwarf war machines may additionally include an Engineer.

• If he part of a Bolt Thrower's crew you may use his BS when firing the Bolt Thrower.

• If he is part of a Grudge Thrower or Cannon's crew and the war machine suffers a Misfire you may re-roll a result on the Misfire chart for that weapon.

ARTILLERY CREW

The artillery crew special rules that follow apply to all Dwarf war machine crews (except the Gyrocopter pilot) and to Master Engineers or Engineers that have joined a war machine as additional crew.

	M	WS	BS	S	T	W	I	A	Ld
Artillery Crew	3	4	3	3	4	1	2	1	9

Gunners' Pride. Dwarfs crewing a war machine are Stubborn as long as the machine they are crewing has not been destroyed. They will be unwilling to leave them unguarded, however, and can never choose to Flee as a charge response or pursue a Fleeing enemy.

Additional Crew. Dwarf Artillery follows the Warhammer rules relating to Loss of Crew. If a war machine has been joined by a Master Engineer and/or Engineer, then they may act as crew. If so, they will suffer the consequences of any Misfire result.

In any given Shooting phase, a Master Engineer or an Engineer who has joined a war machine can either act as additional crew; use their Artillery Master or Artillery Specialist special rules; or fire personal weaponry. They must declare the option they will use before firing the war machine.

FLAME CANNON

A volatile concoction of hot oil and molten tar is mixed in the barrel of the Flame Cannon. Air is pumped into the barrel until the pressure inside is very great and the barrel is almost ready to burst. At precisely the right moment the Dwarfs place a burning oily wad into the nozzle and release the pressure inside. The mixture catches fire as it spurts from the barrel and burning oil arcs into the air towards the enemy ranks. With a bit of luck, the flaming oil lands right in the middle of an enemy unit, spraying fire and boiling tar over the target.

Move	Toughness	Wounds
As crew	7	3

The Flame Cannon can be moved at the speed of its crew as specified for Cannons in the Warhammer rulebook. The Flame Cannon may be turned on the spot to face its target, but cannot otherwise move and fire in the same turn.

Loss of crew. The Flame Cannon is affected by loss of crew as detailed in the main Warhammer rules.

Firing the Flame Cannon.
Flame Cannons shoot in a similar way to cannons, but instead of firing a cannon ball they shoot a gout of flame – use the Flame template to represent this.

Range	Strength	Wounds	Armour Save
12"	5	D3	-2

To fire the cannon, first turn it on the spot so that it points at your intended target. Now declare how far you wish to shoot, up to a maximum of 12", eg, 12", 10", 7", etc. This represents the gunners elevating the barrel to get the required trajectory. The jet of inflammable liquid will travel the distance you have nominated plus the score of an Artillery dice (marked 2, 4, 6, 8, 10 and Misfire).

Roll the Artillery dice and add the score to the distance you have nominated. The jet travels the total distance and will land short, hit the target, or pass over it depending on how accurately you have guessed the range and what effect the dice roll has.

When you have established where the jet of flaming liquid hits the ground, place the Flame template on that spot. The jet sprays out from this point and scorches a line through any targets in its way. To determine the swathe cut by the burning liquid, place the Flame template with the narrow end on the point where the jet hit the ground and the wide end pointing directly away from the cannon so that the flame continues in a straight line. Any models completely under the template are automatically hit and models partially covered are hit on the roll of a 4+. Any model struck by the flame takes a Strength 5 hit and any model wounded by the flame takes D3 wounds. Saving throws apply as normal (ie, -2 Armour Save).

A unit that suffers casualties from the Flame Cannon, must take an immediate Panic test to represent the horrific effects of this weapon.

If you roll a Misfire on the Artillery dice then the Flame Cannon has malfunctioned. Roll a D6 and check the Flame Cannon Misfire chart below to see what happens.

FLAME CANNON MISFIRE CHART

D6 Result

1 **Destroyed!** Smoke begins to pour from the barrel in a worrying fashion and a few seconds later it explodes into a fireball, engulfing everyone nearby. The Flame Cannon is destroyed and its crew slain.

2-3 **Malfunction.** The mixture fails to ignite and the cannon squirts smelly hot oil and tar into the air. Although unpleasant, this is not deadly, and has no effect on the target. The crew must prepare the cannon for firing again, so the Flame Cannon may not shoot this turn or next turn.

4-6 **Phut.** The pressure is not high enough, so the Flame Cannon may not fire this turn.

ORGAN GUN

The Dwarf Engineers Guild has developed a four-barrelled cannon called an Organ Gun or Organ Cannon. Its name derives from the pipes of a musical organ, which the array of barrels resembles. The Organ Cannon's barrels are smaller and lighter than that of an ordinary cannon, which means it lacks the range and hitting power, but the gun does have the advantage of being able to fire several shots at once.

The Organ Gun has more barrels than an ordinary cannon but these are smaller and lighter. Its range and the damage it inflicts are considerably different from a cannon's.

Range	Strength	Armour Save
24"	5	-3

Move	Toughness	Wounds
As crew	7	3

Organ Guns are stoutly made from iron and can sustain considerable damage as shown on their profile. The Organ Gun can be moved at the speed of its crew as specified for Cannons in the Warhammer rulebook. The Organ Gun cannot move and shoot in the same turn, other than to pivot on the spot to face its target.

Loss of crew. The Organ Gun is affected by loss of crew as detailed in the main Warhammer rules.

Firing the Dwarf Organ Gun. In the Shooting phase, nominate a target unit and turn the Organ Gun so that it faces it. Roll the Artillery dice and then measure the range. If the target unit is within range it will suffer a number of hits equal to the number rolled on the Artillery dice. Hits are resolved using the profile below.

If you roll a Misfire, the cannon has misfired and may explode. Roll a D6 and consult the Organ Gun Misfire chart below to see what happens.

Whenever you fire the Organ Gun you may re-roll the Artillery dice if it didn't score a Misfire. If a Misfire results on the re-roll it automatically causes a Fzzz... Clunk result as the gun simply fails to fire.

ORGAN GUN MISFIRE CHART

D6 Result

1-2 Destroyed! The gun explodes with a mighty crack. Shards of metal fly in all directions leaving a hole in the ground, a cloud of black smoke and the stench of burnt beards. The gun is destroyed and its crew slain or injured. Remove the Organ Gun and its crew.

3-4 Malfunction. The gun fails to ignite and does not fire. The crew fuss around, banging it with hammers and muttering to themselves before working out what is wrong. The gun cannot fire this turn or next turn.

5-6 Fzzz... Clunk. A minor fault prevents the gun firing. Perhaps the fuse is not set properly or maybe the young crew mishandled the loading procedure. The Organ Gun does not shoot this turn. However, it is unharmed and may shoot as normal next turn.

CANNON

Only the most expert Engineers have the range of skills needed to make a proper cannon. They can be made quickly in brass, of course, with a simple mould and a wooden frame, but sooner or later they will crack like the shoddy things they are. Only a master can make a gun from steel because only a master can make the machines and tools that will make the cannon. Even then, the finest gun can be betrayed by poor powder. Mixing the components in the right quantities and fixing it so that it detonates consistently is an art in itself. Proving a cannon can take centuries, by which time it is a part of the clan that made it; like a favourite daughter, attention is lavished upon it and the cannon carries their pride on its broad wheels.

Cannons follow the rules given in the Warhammer rulebook. Note that a Dwarf Cannon is the smaller of the two types defined.

GRUDGE THROWER

Grudge Throwers were originally simple stone throwers, used to command the approaches to Dwarf holds. It was during the War of Vengeance that the practice of inscribing grudges on the rocks to be used as ammunition developed, so great was the fury of the Dwarfs at the betrayal of the Elves.

Even after the war there was no peace for the Dwarfs as hold after hold fell to the Greenskins or Rat-men. New chapters were added to the Book of Grudges every year as the Dwarfs fell back to the surviving holds. They brought with them stone fragments of their lost realms and, reviving the older custom, inscribed them with runes describing the injustices done to them and laying curses upon their enemies. During the long siege of Karak Azgul the Dwarfs used these stones as ammunition, literally hurling their grudges back at their enemies. Since then it has become commonplace to carefully select and prepare the stones that are to be fired, with many skilled Engineers espousing their belief that the engine is only as good as the rock it throws.

Grudge Throwers follow the rules for Stone Throwers given in the Warhammer rulebook.

BOLT THROWER

Bolt Throwers are simply larger versions of the crossbow, able to fire heavier bolts over greater distances. Engineers still vie with each other to invent Bolt Throwers with greater range, loading speed or accuracy. Practical to a fault, the Dwarfs place more trust in an old, proven Bolt Thrower that has fired reliably for generations. The Bolt Thrower remains an important part of the Dwarf arsenal because it can be built and maintained cheaply and is accurate enough to bring down monsters such as Wyverns or Trolls with a well-judged shot. Its direct trajectory of fire and uncomplicated mechanism also enable it to be used effectively underground, and without obscuring everything around it in choking smoke.

Bolt Throwers follow the rules given in the Warhammer rulebook.

BATTLE OF BLACK FIRE PASS

When the war chief of the human Unberogen tribe, Sigmar, rescued King Kurgan Ironbeard from Orc captivity, he won himself a powerful ally. As well as being gifted with Ghal Maraz, a rune hammer of considerable power, a military alliance developed between Men and Dwarfs. After raising the siege of Zhufbar, Sigmar again stood alongside King Kurgan to hold Black Fire Pass against a new Orc Waaagh! Men's memories are short, however, and they kept no records. The Dwarf's exploits were recorded by the great Runesmith, Alaric the Mad, and are retained in the Book of the High Kings, the Rikakron.

The Dwarf throng received the first Orc attacks and repelled three great waves. The fourth, however, threatened to overwhelm them but Sigmar unleashed his mounted warriors in a fierce charge that cleared the lines and regained the momentum. Dwarf and Man surged forward, taking the fight to the Orcs but such were the numbers of Greenskins coming down the pass, that they could not be broken as there was nowhere to flee. It was a nightmare of sundered shields and shattered helmets, a claustrophobic press in which Dwarfs, Men and Orcs fought, died and were trodden beneath the boots of the living. The advantage was with the alliance but in the confines of the pass no clear victory could be won.

It was then that the engineers commanding the Dwarf artillery ordered that the crews move their weapons onto a rocky ledge at the side of the pass. Sinews bursting, the Dwarfs hefted their prized weapons up the dangerous slope. Once there, they fired over the thinning ranks of their comrades into the mass of Orcs still coming up the pass. The Orcs were so tightly packed that it was impossible to miss. With such a barrage coming at them out of the dark sky, the Orc reserves first slowed and then began to retreat. This was the final straw. With nothing to hold them in place, the Orcs began to flee. Scarcely any horses remained alive so there could be no cavalry pursuit but in truth it wasn't needed. For two miles, the pass was carpeted with Orc dead. So great was King Kurgan's joy that he allowed Alaric to fashion the Runefang swords that would be the rewards for Sigmar's greatest warriors.

GYROCOPTER

Gyrocopters are flying machines whose rotor blades are propelled by an ingenious lightweight steam engine. These devices can take off and land vertically or even hover on the spot. Gyrocopters were invented by the Dwarf Engineers Guild and are flown by members of the guild. It is easy to see why Dwarfs invented these machines when you consider their high mountain realm. The inventor was probably inspired by watching dragons swooping down from mountain crags and combined the idea of wings with that of engines used to drive drilling machines and flywheels from grinding machines! Gyrocopters can take off and land easily amid the peaks, as the lofty pinnacles make excellent landing points.

Gyrocopters enable strongholds to keep in contact by flying directly over the difficult mountain passes which may be infested with enemies. Supplies and messages can be dropped from a Gyrocopter directly onto a beleaguered Dwarf settlement, enabling them to hold out for longer and send word for help. In battle, Gyrocopters provide Dwarf armies with the speed and ability to strike anywhere that they lack since they do not use mounted troops.

A Gyrocopter is a unique device that combines some of the qualities of a war machine with those of a flying unit.

	M	WS	BS	S	T	W	I	A	Ld
Gyrocopter	-	4	-	4	5	3	2	2	9

Gyrocopters have a Unit Strength of 3. They are considered to be war machines only insofar that they are affected by spells or magical effects that specifically affect war machines. Each Gyrocopter deploys as a separate unit and does not have to be deployed with other war machines. In all other respects it is treated as a Flying monster.

If the Gyrocopter can't fly for any reason, it can't move.

A Gyrocopter that chooses to flee as a charge reaction and subsequently rallies at the beginning of its next turn may reform facing in any direction and is free to move during the Movement phase, but may not shoot or charge.

Armour Save. The Gyrocopter has a 4+ Armour Save.

Steam Gun. The Gyrocopter is armed with a steam-powered gun that unleashes a hail of lead bullets similar to a cannon's grapeshot. To represent the blast of the steam gun, use the Flame template. Place the template with the broad end over the target and the narrow end touching the muzzle of the gun. Any models completely under the template are automatically hit and models partially covered are hit on the roll of a 4+. You may not Stand & Shoot with a steam gun.

Range	Strength	Armour Save
Flame Template	3	-1

DWARF RUNES

Dwarfs are extremely resistant to magic and its influence, neither perceiving its presence nor feeling its effects. They have learned to use the power of magic in a different way to other races, by incorporating it into magic items such as hammers, axes and armour. The Dwarfs are the greatest and most successful of all races when it comes to making magic items. Indeed, many of the most powerful magic weapons used by Elves and Men were made by the Dwarfs.

A Dwarf who makes magic items is called a Runesmith. As Dwarfs have no direct equivalent to a Human wizard, he is a very important individual. The Runesmiths are an ancient guild of craftsmen, and for thousands of years they have preserved the secrets of how to forge magic runes with incredible power.

The Dwarf language is written in runes, inscriptions specifically designed to be carved in stone or engraved in metal. Magic runes are different to ordinary runes in shape and detail, but much of what makes a rune magical is how and when it is engraved. Magic runes trap magical power – their presence binds and holds magic just as a nail holds together two pieces of timber. Most simple Dwarf runes can trap weak amounts of magic if engraved in a special way, but magic runes can entrap much greater power. Such runes include the awesome master runes and certain secret runes known only to Runesmiths of the temples of Grungni, Grimnir and Valaya.

RUNIC MAGIC

Runic magic items are effectively magic items tailored to your own requirements by combining different abilities.

A Dwarf character can carry runic magic items and the total points value of these runic items is limited in the same way as normal.

It is important to remember that a runic item is no different in principle to any other magic item, and all the usual rules for magic items still apply. For example, if a creature cannot be harmed by an ordinary weapon but can be harmed by a magic weapon, then obviously a runic weapon will affect it too. All the rules that apply to the possession and use of magic items also apply to runic magic items.

CREATING A RUNE ITEM

Runes can be inscribed onto any of the following things: weapons, armour, standards, war machines and talismans. Each of these has its own type of runes.

The easiest way to create a runic item is to choose a character from your army – a Dwarf Thane armed with an axe, for example. By inscribing runes onto his axe you will be, in effect, arming him with a magic weapon — a rune axe. You can choose which rune you want from the weapon runes detailed in this section. Each rune has a specific points value; the more powerful the rune, the higher the points cost. You can put up to three runes onto a weapon, paying the appropriate cost each time.

Once you have chosen the runes you want, write down the Thane's name and note that he has a rune axe with the runes you have selected. Note down the total points cost of the runes you have used and add this to the character's points value. You should make a list of all your characters that are using runic items so that you can refer to it during the battle. It is a good idea to make a brief note of what each rune does, as this will save you looking up details during play.

NUMBER OF RUNIC ITEMS

A character may have no more than one runic item from each of the five categories (ie, one runic weapon, one runic armour, one runic talisman, etc). Remember, a character with a magic weapon can't use other mêlée weapons but can be armed with a crossbow, a handgun or a pistol in addition to a runic mêlée weapon. If armed with a pistol, it may not be used along with a runic mêlée weapon to give +1 Attack.

CHOOSING RUNES

There are many types of rune, all of which bestow a special power or bonus. By combining runes together in different ways, you can create devices of great power. The most powerful runes are very expensive; others are cheaper.

It is up to you to decide how to use runes. It is the ability to tailor your magic items to your foe or to your tactics that makes runic magic items so uniquely useful.

RULES OF THE RUNES

You may inscribe up to three runes on a runic magic item, subject to the following restrictions:

1) No item can have more than three runes. It is virtually impossible to forge items able to bear the strain of carrying so much power. Runesmiths call this the **Rule of Three**.

2) Weapon runes can only be inscribed on weapons, armour runes can only be inscribed on armour, runic standards can only be inscribed on standards, engineering runes can only be inscribed on war machines, and talismanic runes can only be inscribed on talismans (of which more later). This is called the **Rule of Form** by Runesmiths.

3) No more than one item may carry the same combination of magic runes. You could not have two rune weapons both engraved with a Rune of Speed and a Rune of Fire, for example. This restriction also applies to the use of single runes, so you could not have two characters in your army wearing armour engraved with a single Rune of Resistance, for example. Creating rune items takes a great deal of effort and Runesmiths don't like repeating themselves. Nor do they copy other Runesmiths' work, except during their apprenticeship. This is known among Runesmiths as the **Rule of Pride**.

4) No master rune may be used more than once per army, and no more than one master rune can be inscribed on an item. Master runes are so powerful that they cannot be combined together on the same item or used together on the same battlefield. For this reason, Runesmiths describe these runes as **Jealous Runes**.

5) Apart from the master runes (which can only be used once) other runes can be combined as you wish to produce varied or cumulative effects. For example, you might inscribe a weapon with the Master Rune of Swiftness (always strikes first), the Rune of Striking (+1 Weapon Skill) and the Rune of Fury (+1 Attack). With the exception of master runes, runes can be used in multiples, in which case their effects are added together. For example, you could inscribe a weapon with the Rune of Fury (+1 Attack) three times to give you +3 Attacks.

WEAPON RUNES

Weapon runes are inscribed onto hammers or axes to turn them into runic weapons. Note that although Dwarfs may inscribe runes on weapons, none of the bonuses/penalties for the original weapon apply. The fact that the weapon is magical supersedes any normal rules for such weapons. There is one exception to this – see the Master Rune of Kragg the Grim.

MASTER RUNE OF SKALF BLACKHAMMER   75 points

The legendary Runesmith Skalf forged many great hammers, and some say even Sigmar's hammer was his work. Many of his hammers were later held by Dwarf Lords as heirlooms of their kingship.

A weapon bearing this rune will strike with adequate strength to wound the target on a score of 2+ based on the target's Toughness. This Strength is also used as a modifier to Armour Saves against the weapon. For example, against a Toughness 4 target, Strength 6 is needed to wound on a 2+, so the Save modifier is -3.

MASTER RUNE OF SMITING   70 points

This rune was previously only known on the Axe of Dargo wielded by the Kings of Karak Kadrin. Prior to marching out to face Vardek Crom, King Ungrim Ironfist gifted the Rundrokikron, an ancient tome of rune lore, etched on wafer sheets of gromril, to Thorgrim Grudgebearer, the King of Karaz-a-Karak. Within it was the secret of striking the Master Rune of Smiting.

An enemy wounded by a weapon with the Master Rune of Smiting (after Saves, etc) takes not 1 but D6 wounds.

MASTER RUNE OF ALARIC THE MAD   50 points

No one knows exactly what happened to Alaric the Mad after he forged the famous Runefangs of the Elector Counts of the Empire, though some say he wrought rune weapons for the Khan Queens of Kislev.

When wounded by this weapon, the target is not allowed an Armour Saving throw.

MASTER RUNE OF BREAKING   45 points

First used during the War of Vengeance, this rune was inscribed upon King Gorrin's axe, which destroyed the High Elf General Elthior's enchanted blade. It has become a popularly used rune ever since.

If the Dwarf character scores a hit against an enemy with a magic weapon, the enemy's magic weapon is destroyed immediately.

MASTER RUNE OF FLIGHT   40 points

The original inscription for this rune did not specify that the hammer return to the wielder's hand, and many Dwarfs found themselves knocked unconscious as their own weapons returned to them.

May not be used by Slayer characters. A weapon with the Master Rune of Flight functions exactly as a thrown weapon with a range of 12", with the exception that it may target any enemy model within line of sight of the wielder that is not involved in a close combat. The target is automatically hit once as if the two models were in close combat (thus any additional runes on the weapon take effect), then the hammer flies back into the wielder's hand.

In addition, a weapon with this rune may be used in close combat as a hand weapon, although this rune has no effect in close combat beyond making the hand weapon magical.

RUNE OF MIGHT   25 points

Though short in stature, a Dwarf using a weapon inscribed with this rune is a powerful opponent.

Multiples of this rune have no further effect. The wielder's Strength is doubled against any enemies with Toughness 5 or more.

MASTER RUNE OF SWIFTNESS   25 points

First struck by Thurgrom the Hermit, the last Runesmith to work in the Elf cities of the Old World.

A weapon engraved with this rune always strikes first, even against chargers. In situations where both sides are entitled to strike first, the highest Initiative value has priority over the lower value. If Initiatives are equal, follow the Who Strikes First rules for resolving ties. See the Warhammer rulebook for details.

RUNE OF SNORRI SPANGELHELM   25 points

Runesmith to the High King of Karaz-a-Karak during the time of Kallon, Snorri wrought the exquisite war panoply of the High Kings for several generations. He fought in many battles and was renowned for his magnificent gromril armour as well as this unique weapon rune.

Any blows struck by a weapon engraved with this rune are at +1 to hit. Multiple runes are cumulative, but cannot reduce the score needed to hit to less than 2.

RUNE OF FURY   25 points

The Dwarf wielding the weapon must concentrate upon an unavenged grudge, causing him to become enraged at the wrongs his race has endured.

The wielder of this weapon adds +1 to his Attack characteristic.

RUNE OF CLEAVING   20 points

This rune was originally forged upon the pickaxes of miners, enabling them to break through the hardest rock.

The wielder of this weapon adds +1 to his Strength.

MASTER RUNE OF KRAGG THE GRIM   20 points

This rune was commonplace in the past but its secrets had been lost to the centuries. However, Dwarf adventurers in Karak Azgal discovered several axes bearing the rune and carried one to Karaz-a-Karak where it came into the possession of the Master Runesmith, Kragg the Grim. By dint of long study, Kragg came to understand the secrets of the rune and how to inscribe it. The jealous old Runelord might have kept the secret to himself but, knowing that other Runesmiths were probably studying it, elected to share the knowledge and thereby gained the credit for deciphering the secret.

This rune can only be placed on great weapons. It allows the great weapon to retain its normal abilities (+2 Strength, strike last etc).

GRUDGE RUNE   15 points

Often an enemy's misdeeds are so great that a Dwarf will have this rune put upon his weapon and will not rest until his foe pays for his wrongs with blood.

Multiples of this rune have no further effect. Nominate one enemy character or monster at the beginning of the game by secretly noting it on your roster. The wielder may re-roll misses in close combat when attacking this enemy model.

RUNE OF STRIKING   10 points

The properties of this rune enable the weapon's wielder to find an enemy's weak points with ease.

The wielder of this weapon may add +1 to his Weapon Skill.

RUNE OF SPEED   5 points

This rune enhances the Dwarf's awareness, allowing him to pick his targets far quicker.

The wielder of this weapon adds +1 to his Initiative.

RUNE OF FIRE   5 points

A skilled Runesmith is able to inscribe this rune on the metal while it is still white hot from the forge.

The weapon makes Flaming attacks.

ARMOUR RUNES

These runes are the most powerful protective magic known to the Dwarfs. They are inscribed only on armour. Any Dwarf character may be given up to three armour runes.

MASTER RUNE OF STEEL   50 points

Once this rune has been forged, it binds metals together making them more resilient. Armour with this rune never rusts through weathering or age.

Attacks against the bearer of this rune with a Strength greater than 5 are treated as Strength 5.

RUNE OF FORTITUDE   50 points

It is rumoured amongst those Dwarfs who have worn armour with this rune that it becomes sentient. Whilst no Runesmith has ever confirmed this rumour, they make no attempts to deny it either.

This rune gives its bearer +1 Wound.

MASTER RUNE OF ADAMANT   45 points

First forged on armour as a gift for the flamboyant Dwarf Prince Gudii Twoboots, the armour was subsequently stolen by a lone bandit who stalked the Undgrim preying on small parties of travellers.

This rune adds +1 to the Toughness of the character.

MASTER RUNE OF GROMRIL   25 points

A small amount of pure gromril is the most important element used when inscribing this rune. If the sample is even slightly flawed, the rune will not work.

Confers a 1+ Armour Save that cannot be improved in any way.

RUNE OF SHIELDING   25 points

This rune was created during the War of Vengeance as a protection against the missile fire of the High Elves.

Multiples of this rune have no further effect. The character has a 2+ Ward Save against shooting attacks and spells defined as Magic Missiles.

RUNE OF RESISTANCE   25 points

First used on the armour of the Thane of Karak Azgal by Gorgi Strongbeard, this rune is thought to have been lost amongst the ruined stronghold. Fortunately, the Runesmith survived to replicate it.

Multiples of this rune have no further effect. This rune allows the character to re-roll any failed Armour Saving throws.

RUNE OF IRON   15 points

When iron is saturated with magic, it is known as lodestone. This rune focuses the magnetic properties of lodestone to create magical armour.

This rune confers a 6+ Ward Save. Two of these runes confer a 5+ Ward Save, but three cannot be taken, because only the Master Rune of Spite can bind such huge power.

RUNE OF PRESERVATION   15 points

When Prince Valkan Firehand was decapitated by a Wight Blade at the Battle of Hunger Wood, many Runesmiths and armourers were alarmed at an apparent weakness in Dwarf armour. Their answer was to use rune magic to add extra protection to those parts of the armour that could not be made any thicker.

Multiples of this rune have no further effect. This rune confers immunity to the Killing Blow and Poisoned Attack rules. Attacks aimed at this model are resolved as if the attacker did not have either ability.

RUNE OF STONE   5 points

Dwarf tradition tells that the ancients were created from the rock of the first mountains, so the Rune of Stone is the first rune an apprentice learns.

Multiples of this rune have no further effect. This rune adds +1 to the character's Armour Save. The Rune of Stone is an exception to the normal Rule of Pride that forbids the same combination of runes to be used on several items, so a single Rune of Stone may be inscribed onto any character's armour.

RUNIC STANDARDS

These runes may be inscribed on standards and can offer the entire unit protection from psychology and magic. They may also be inscribed on the Battle Standard. Master runes are placed upon Battle Standards by Runesmiths under the supervision of priests of the temples of Grungni, Grimnir and Valaya.

MASTER RUNE OF VALAYA   100 points

This ancient rune is said to have been invented at the dawn of time by Valaya, the Ancestor Goddess.

This rune adds +2 to all attempts to dispel made by the owning player. Any spell that remains in play is dispelled automatically at the start of either player's Magic phase if the target it affects is within 12" of the standard. For example, a Wall of Fire will be dispelled if it is within 12" of the standard.

MASTER RUNE OF STROMNI REDBEARD   100 points

Stromni Redbeard made this rune in the days of Bael, Lord of Karak Azul. It was first carved onto the battle standard of Durgin, son of Grindol, son of Grimnir.

This rune adds a further +1 to the combat result of all combats involving at least one friendly Dwarf unit that is within 12" of it.

MASTER RUNE OF FEAR   75 points

The clan that takes this banner to battle gives the illusion that they tower over the enemy. Dwarfs are a strong enough opponent in their own right but a unit of giant Dwarfs is enough to scare even the strongest enemy!

The unit causes *fear*.

STROLLAZ'S RUNE   55 points

This rune harnesses the tireless nature of the Dwarfs, enabling them to march day and night. So powerful is the magic that the trick is often stopping them marching.

Multiples of this rune have no further effect. After deployment, but before the dice roll to determine first turn, any and all friendly Dwarf units (except Gyrocopters) within 12" of the Banner may make an immediate move. This may be a march but cannot be a charge. Any units that make this move count as having moved during turn one for the purposes of shooting.

MASTER RUNE OF GRUNGNI   50 points

This rune draws in the power of the winds of magic and binds them into the armour of the Dwarfs in its vicinity, granting protection against the direst weapons.

Any friendly Dwarf unit within 6" of a standard with this rune gets a 5+ Ward Save against shooting attacks and any spell defined as Magic Missiles.

RUNE OF SLOWNESS   50 points

This rune creates an almost physical barrier from the intractable nature of the Dwarfs around it.

Any foes charging the unit subtract D6" from their charge distance. If the unit fails to make contact then all the usual rules for a failed charge apply. If multiples of this rune are used, the charge reduction is not added up, instead roll a D6 for each rune and choose the best score.

RUNE OF COURAGE   30 points

Resonating with the power of duty and loyalty, this rune further bolsters the resolve of Dwarfs near it.

Multiples of this rune have no further effect. The unit is immune to *fear* and *terror*.

RUNE OF GUARDING   30 points

It is no easy task to carry a hold's banner into battle, for every enemy warrior dreams of the glory of capturing it. This rune defends the bearer of the standard.

Army Standard Bearer only. Multiples of this rune have no further effect. The bearer of a standard with the Rune of Guarding has a 5+ Ward Save.

RUNE OF BATTLE   25 points

Each of the Dwarf strongholds once had a banner with the Rune of Battle upon it. Many of these banners are now lost, but those that still remain in Dwarf hands are held aloft with pride.

Multiples of this rune have no further effect. The unit adds a further +1 to its combat result score.

RUNE OF STOICISM   25 points

This rune reminds every Dwarf that though their numbers diminish, each carries the legacy of their ancestors with them and they are never alone.

Multiples of this rune have no further effect. The unit counts as double its actual Unit Strength.

RUNE OF DETERMINATION   20 points

Even in the most hopeless struggle, it is not within the heart of a Dwarf to concede defeat. The Rune of Determination magnifies that spirit when it is most severely tested.

One use only. Multiples of this rune have no further effect. The unit may take a Break test on a single D6 rather than 2D6.

RUNE OF SANCTUARY   15 points

This rune creates an area of anti-magic, using the defiance of the Dwarfs to deflect mystical attacks.

Each rune confers Magic Resistance (1) to the unit.

ANCESTOR RUNE   10 points

In adversity, Dwarfs can look to the runes of their ancestors and remember the duty they bear.

One use only. If the unit carrying a banner with this rune has to take a Break test, the rune is expended. Roll a D6. On a roll of 4+ the unit, and any character that has joined it, tests as if it were Stubborn. Only one rune may be expended per Break test taken.

RUNIC TALISMANS

Talismanic runes can be inscribed upon amulets, belts, crowns, helms and other ornamental pieces, though they are most commonly found on rings. Every character is assumed to already have the relevant item in his possession.

MASTER RUNE OF KINGSHIP   100 points

Gotrek Starbreaker was the first great Dwarf Lord to have his crown adorned with this rune. Such a crown is a priceless artefact and the loss of one is dearly mourned as it absorbs the wisdom of its former master and passes this on to the next crown bearer.

This rune may only be engraved on the crown of a Dwarf Lord. The Lord and the unit he leads are Stubborn and immune to *fear* and *terror*.

MASTER RUNE OF BALANCE   50 points

Forged in the embers of a captured spell book, this rune hungers after magical power, stealing it from the enemy.

Runesmiths/Runelords only. During the enemy's Magic phase, this rune allows the owning player to remove one dice from the opponent's pile of Power dice and add it to his own Dispel dice pile.

MASTER RUNE OF SPELLBINDING   50 points

This rune allows a Runesmith to channel away the winds of magic with greater ease, thwarting the magical attacks of their foes.

Runesmiths/Runelords only. This rune gives +1 to all attempts to dispel made by the owning player.

SPELLEATER RUNE   50 points

This rune makes Runesmiths and Runelords almost invulnerable to magical attacks.

Runesmiths/Runelords only. One use only. This rune works exactly like a Rune of Spellbreaking (see below). Also, when the enemy spell is cancelled, roll a dice. On the roll of a 4+, the enemy spell is lost to the Wizard casting it and can't be cast again by him for the rest of the game.

MASTER RUNE OF SPITE   45 points

Created to protect the gates of Karaz-a-Karak, this rune has since been transferred onto other devices.

This rune confers a 4+ Ward Save.

RUNE OF FATE   35 points

A Dwarf possessing this rune will dream portents of the future the night before a battle, and he will know each blow that the enemy will strike at him.

Multiples of this rune have no further effect. One use only. The model has a 2+ Ward Save against the first wound suffered and not saved by armour.

MASTER RUNE OF CHALLENGE   25 points

A foe that bears this rune is suddenly aware of the challenge issued by the Dwarf sounding it as well as the indomitable will that powers it. The only options that remain are fight or flight.

One use only. This rune is normally inscribed in a book or on a warhorn. The rune is used during the enemy turn before they declare charges. Nominate one enemy unit within 20" of the rune user. The unit must be able to charge and reach the rune user or the unit he is with according to the normal rules. The enemy unit must either declare a charge against the rune user (and any unit he is with) or must flee in the Compulsory Movement phase as if it had failed a Panic test. This rune has no effect on units that are Immune to Psychology.

MASTER RUNE OF DISMAY   25 points

When a warhorn with this rune is sounded, its uncanny voice causes all foes to tremble.

One use only. This rune is normally inscribed in a book or on a warhorn. The rune is used during the enemy turn before they declare charges. All enemy units on the table which are not Immune to Psychology must take a Leadership test. If they fail, they are so dismayed that they may not declare a charge that turn. Units that move in the Compulsory Movement phase are not affected.

RUNE OF SPELLBREAKING   25 points

Once a Runesmith has mastered the Rune of Warding he will learn this more complex rune.

Runesmiths/Runelords only. One use only. This rune will stop enemy magic instantly. The rune may be played to automatically dispel one enemy spell – there is no need to roll. This rune won't help against spells cast with Irresistible Force.

RUNE OF BROTHERHOOD   20 points

This rune allows a Dwarf to quickly assimilate skills possessed by his closest comrades.

Multiples of this rune have no further effect. One Use Only. May not be used by a character with an Oath stone or Shieldbearers. A character with this rune may either be deployed with a unit of Rangers utilising the Scout rule as if he had the Scout rule himself or join a unit of Miners utilising the Underground Advance rule, arriving with them.

RUNE OF LUCK   15 points

First inscribed on a ring worn by Magnund Hammerson, who then went on to acquire a fortune through gambling.

One use only. This rune allows its bearer to re-roll any single to hit roll, to wound roll, Armour Save or Ward Save during the game.

RUNE OF WARDING   15 points

Apprentice Runesmiths are taught the techniques necessary to create this rune early in their studies.

Each rune confers a cumulative Magic Resistance (1) on the character and the unit he is with.

RUNE OF THE FURNACE   5 points

Designed to aid Dwarfs working in the hot forges, this rune was soon adapted for use in battle.

The bearer of this rune is immune to fire and cannot be affected by enemy attacks purely consisting of flaming attacks such as Fire Balls, flames from a Skaven Warpfire Thrower, breath of a High Elf Dragon, etc.

ENGINEERING RUNES

Dwarf Cannons, Grudge Throwers and Bolt Throwers may be inscribed with up to three of the engineering runes described below. The newfangled (to the Dwarfs!) Organ Gun, Flame Cannon and Gyrocopter may not have engineering runes. Note that a shot from a war machine inscribed with any engineering runes counts as a magical attack.

MASTER RUNE OF DEFENCE   40 points

Developed as a defensive measure during the War of Vengeance against the firepower of the High Elves, this rune has saved the lives of many crew.

The war machine and its crew are always assumed to be in hard cover to enemy shooting.

RUNE OF FORGING   35 points

When making a cannon, with each hammer blow an Engineer strikes, a Runesmith must recite a special litany. This can take weeks to complete.

Multiples of this rune have no further effect. Can only be placed on a Cannon. Allows the owning player to re-roll the Artillery dice when he rolls a Misfire. If you roll a Misfire when rolling the Artillery dice either to hit or to bounce, then you can roll again, but you are bound by the second roll even if it's another Misfire.

MASTER RUNE OF DISGUISE   30 points

This rune magically distorts space around the machine, rendering it almost invisible.

Until it moves or shoots, the machine cannot be seen, and cannot therefore be targeted with spells, shot at or charged. Once the machine has moved/fired, or if an enemy unit moves to within 3" of it, the machine is revealed and can be seen and attacked as normal for the rest of the battle.

MASTER RUNE OF IMMOLATION   30 points

Devised to stop machines falling to the enemy, it is invoked only in desperate circumstances.

One use only. The Dwarf player can cause the machine to explode at the end of any round of combat before determining the result. The machine and its crew are all killed. Each enemy unit in combat with the war machine takes 2D6 Strength 4 magical hits allocated as shooting.

MASTER RUNE OF SKEWERING   30 points

Elf mages helped create this before the War of the Beard. There's no mention of this in Dwarf records.

One use only. This rune may only be inscribed on a Bolt Thrower. Once per game the Bolt Thrower hits on a 2+ with no modifiers. You must choose to use this rune before rolling to hit.

RUNE OF ACCURACY   25 points

Once a missile inscribed with this rune is launched, the rune glows, invoking the winds of magic to blow the stone in the right direction.

Multiples of this rune have no further effect. May only be put on a Grudge Thrower. The Dwarf player may re-roll the Scatter dice if he wishes (Note: Only the Scatter dice, not the Artillery dice), enabling the machine to shoot more accurately. If you re-roll the dice, you must accept the result of the second roll.

RUNE OF FORTUNE   25 points

Discovered by Magnus Hammerson, who broke Runesmith tradition by selling it to the Engineers Guild.

One use only. If a machine has the Rune of Fortune, the player may use it to amend a dice rolled on the machine's Misfire chart to a result of 6.

RUNE OF PENETRATING   25 points

This rune is inscribed onto the war machine's ammunition, making it more hard hitting.

The Strength of a hit from the war machine increases by +1, to a maximum of 10.

VALIANT RUNE   20 points

Dwarf crews are famed for always defending their machines to the bitter end when attacked.

As long as their war machine is not destroyed, the war machine crew and any Master Engineer character joined to it are Unbreakable.

STALWART RUNE   20 points

Many Dwarfs believe that a machine with this rune on it will last forever.

This rune adds +1 to the crew's combat resolution score.

FLAKKSON'S RUNE OF SEEKING   15 points

This rune makes Bolt Throwers deadly against flyers by magically directing the bolts to their target.

Bolt Throwers only. Each rune adds +1 to the Bolt Thrower's to hit rolls against targets with the Fly special ability but cannot reduce the score to hit below 2+.

RUNE OF RELOADING   10 points

When a war machine has proved its worth, it may be empowered with this rune.

The war machine can shoot every turn, as long as there is at least one crewman left, even if the machine has rolled a Misfire in the previous turn.

RUNE OF BURNING   5 points

Any ammunition shot by the machine bursts into flames as it hits its target.

The war machine makes Flaming attacks.

FORCES OF THE DWARFS

The purpose of an army list is to enable players with vastly different armies to stage games that are as fair and as evenly balanced as it is possible to make them. The army list gives each individual model a points value which represents its capabilities on the tabletop. The higher a model's points value, the better it is in one or more respects: stronger, tougher, faster, a better leader, and so on. The value of the army is simply the value of all the models added together.

As well as providing points costs, the list divides the army into its constituent units and describes the weapons and optional equipment that troops can have and occasionally restricts the number of very powerful units an army can include. It would be very silly indeed if an army were to consist entirely of thundering Cannons or crazed Daemon Slayers. The resultant game would be a frustrating and unbalanced affair if not a complete waste of time. We employ army lists to ensure that this does not happen!

USING THE ARMY LIST

The army lists enable two players to choose armies of equal points value to fight a battle, as described in the main body of the Warhammer rules. The following list has been constructed with this purpose in mind.

The list can also be used when playing specific scenarios, either those described in the Warhammer rulebook, or others, including ones invented by the players. In this case, the list provides a framework that the players can adapt as required. It might, for example, be felt necessary to increase or decrease the number of characters or units allowed, or to restrict or remove options in the standard list such as certain runes or specific weapons. If you refer to the Scenarios section of the Warhammer rulebook, you'll find some examples of this kind.

ARMY LIST ORGANISATION

The army list is divided into four sections:

CHARACTERS
Representing the most able, skilled and ancient individuals in your army, characters are extraordinary leaders such as Thanes and Runesmiths. These form a vital and potent part of your forces.

CORE UNITS
These represent the most common warriors. They usually form the bulk of the army and will often bear the brunt of the fighting.

SPECIAL UNITS
This category includes the best of your warriors and common engines of war. They are available to your army in limited numbers.

RARE UNITS
So called because they are scarce compared to your ordinary troops. They represent unique units, uncommon creatures and unusual machines.

CHOOSING AN ARMY

Both players choose armies to the same agreed points value. Most players find that 2,000 points is about right for a battle that will last over an evening. Whatever value you agree, this is the maximum number of points you can spend on your army. You can spend less and will probably find it is impossible to use up every last point. Most 2,000 point armies will therefore be something like 1,998 points or 1,999 points, but they still count as 2,000 point armies for our purposes.

Once you have decided on a total points value, it is time to choose your force.

Choosing Characters

Characters are divided into two broad categories: Lords (the most powerful characters) and Heroes (the rest). The maximum number of characters an army can include is shown on the chart below.

Army Points Value	Max. Total Characters	Max. Lords	Max. Heroes
Less than 2,000	3	0	3
2,000 or more	4	1	4
3,000 or more	6	2	6
4,000 or more	8	3	8
Each +1,000	+2	+1	+2

An army does not have to include the maximum number of characters allowed, it can always include fewer than indicated. However, an army must always include at least one character: the General. An army does not have to include Lords – it can include all of its characters as Heroes if you prefer. At the beginning of the battle, choose one of the characters to be the General and make sure that you let your opponent know which one it is.

For example, a 2,500 point army could include a Runelord (Lord), a Thane (Hero), a Runesmith (Hero), and a Dragon Slayer (Hero) (ie, four characters in total, of which one is a Lord).

Choosing Troops

Troops are divided into Core, Special and Rare units. The number of each type of unit available depends on the army's points value, indicated on the chart below.

Army Points Value	Core Units	Special Units	Rare Units
Less than 2,000	2+	0-3	0-1
2,000 or more	3+	0-4	0-2
3,000 or more	4+	0-5	0-3
4,000 or more	5+	0-6	0-4
Each +1,000	+1 min	+0-1	+0-1

In some cases, other limitations may apply to a particular kind of unit. This is specified in the unit entry.

Unit Entries

Each unit is represented by an entry in the army list. The unit's name is given and any limitations that apply are explained.

Profiles. The characteristic profiles for the troops in each unit are given in the unit entry. Where several profiles are required, these are also given even if, as in many cases, they are optional.

Unit Sizes. Each entry specifies the minimum size for each unit. In the case of Core units, this is usually ten models. In the case of other units it is usually less. There are exceptions as you will see. In some cases, units also have a maximum size.

Weapons and Armour. Each entry lists the standard weapons and armour for that unit type. The cost of these items is included in the basic points value. Additional or optional weapons and armour cost extra and are covered in the Options section of the unit entry.

Options. Many entries list the different weapon, armour and equipment options for the unit and any additional points cost for taking them. It may also include the option to upgrade a unit member to a Champion. While this model usually has a specific name (the Champion of a Miner unit is called a Prospector, for example) all the rules that apply to Champions apply to them.

Special Rules. Many troops have special rules which are fully described elsewhere in this book. These rules are also summarised for your convenience in the army list.

It would be a long and tedious business to repeat all the special rules for every unit within the army list itself. The army list is intended primarily as a tool for choosing armies rather than for presenting game rules. Wherever possible we have indicated where special rules apply and, where space permits, we have provided notes within the list as 'memory joggers'. Bear in mind that these descriptions are not necessarily exhaustive or definitive and players should refer to the main Warhammer rulebook for a full account.

Dogs of War

Dogs of War are troops of other races prepared to fight in return for money, food, or some other reward. The most common type of Dogs of War units are the Regiments of Renown. The two terms are both used to describe mercenary units, both work in the same way in the army list.

A selection of such regiments is available as part of the Dogs of War range of models. The descriptions and rules for these units can be found in White Dwarf magazine and are compiled on the Games Workshop web site.

The rules for individual Regiments of Renown detail exactly which armies may take them and which army list choices they use up. Most Dogs of War units take up a Rare choice, but some count as Special choices, or may take up more than one choice. This is detailed in the individual rules of the unit itself.

LORDS

Dwarf Lords (Lords, Runelords and Daemon Slayers) are the most ancient and powerful characters in the Dwarf list.

Dwarf Lords are limited in number and expensive, but make the best army Generals.

0-1 ANVIL OF DOOM

A Runelord can bring into battle the holy Anvil of Doom. This takes up a Hero choice in addition to his Lord choice. The Anvil is accompanied by two Anvil Guards (see pages 30-31), each with the following profile:

	M	WS	BS	S	T	W	I	A	Ld
Anvil Guard	3	5	3	4	4	1	2	1	9

Equipment
Hand weapon, gromril armour & shield.

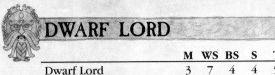

DWARF LORD   Points/model: 145

	M	WS	BS	S	T	W	I	A	Ld
Dwarf Lord	3	7	4	4	5	3	4	4	10

Equipment: Hand weapon and gromril armour.

Options:

• May choose either a great weapon (+6 points), or a pistol (+10 points).

• May also choose either a crossbow (+10 points), or a Dwarf handgun (+15 points).

• May carry a shield (+3 points).

• May choose runic items from the Weapons, Armour and Talisman lists (pages 44-47) with a maximum total value of 125 points.

• May have an Oath stone (+30 points) or if the Lord is the army's General he may be carried into battle by Shieldbearers (+25 points).

Special Rule
Royal Blood

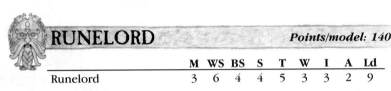

RUNELORD   Points/model: 140

	M	WS	BS	S	T	W	I	A	Ld
Runelord	3	6	4	4	5	3	3	2	9

Equipment: Hand weapon and gromril armour.

Options:

• May be armed with a great weapon (+6 points).

• May carry a shield (+3 points).

• One Runelord in an army may bring an Anvil of Doom to battle (+175 points). The Anvil of Doom comes with two Anvil Guards as shown to the left. If this option is chosen, the Runelord will also take up an extra Hero choice.

• May choose runic items from the Weapons, Armour and Talisman lists (pages 44-47) with a maximum total value of 150 points.

Special Rule
Rune Lore

DAEMON SLAYER   Points/model: 110

	M	WS	BS	S	T	W	I	A	Ld
Daemon Slayer	3	7	3	4	5	3	5	4	10

Equipment: Slayer axes.

Options:

• May choose runic items from the Weapons list (page 44), with a maximum total value of 100 points.

Special Rules
Slayer; Unbreakable; Loner; Slayer Axes

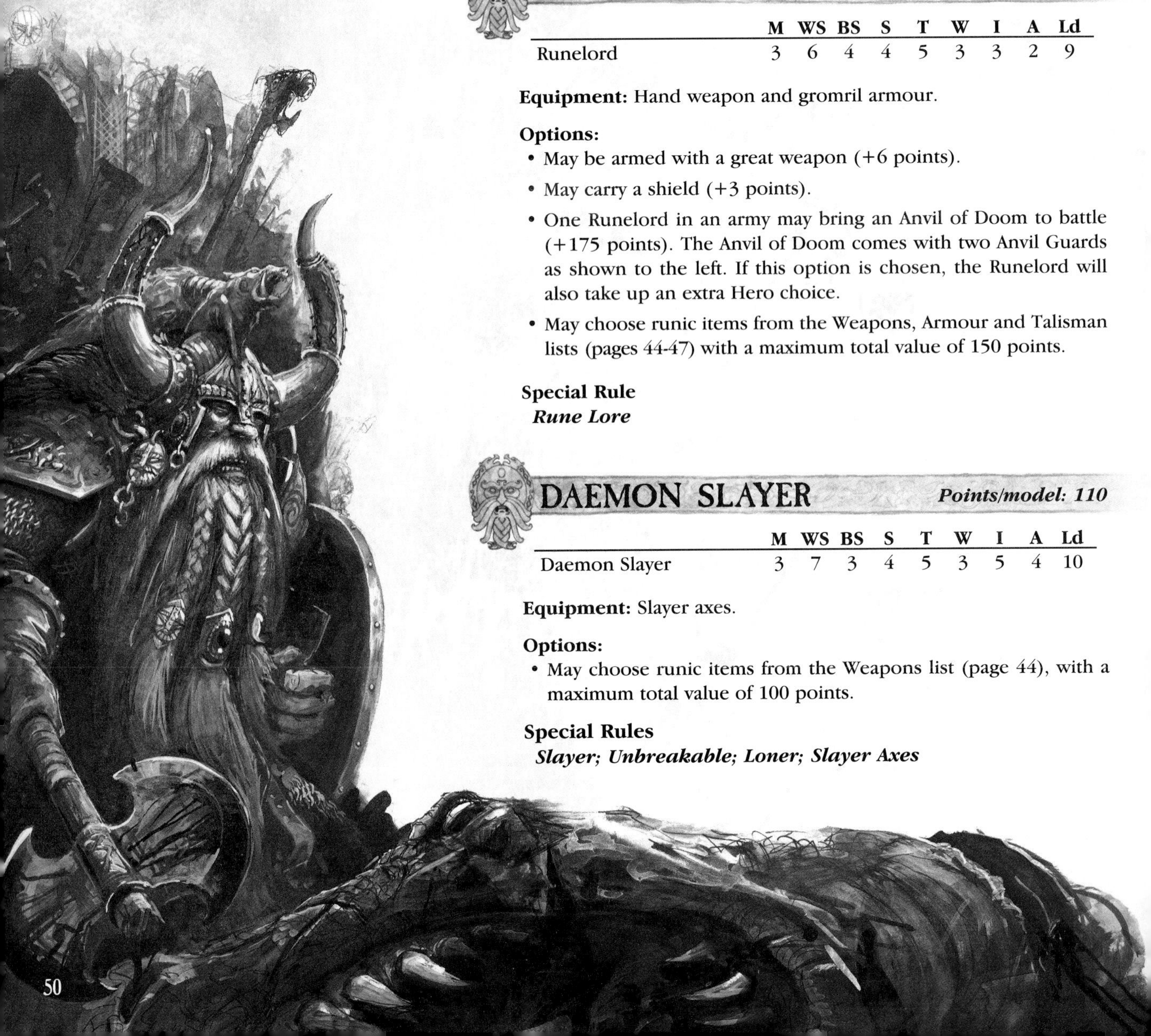

THANE *
Points/model: 65

	M	WS	BS	S	T	W	I	A	Ld
Thane	3	6	4	4	5	2	3	3	9

Equipment: Hand weapon and gromril armour.

Options:
- May choose either a great weapon (+4 points), or a pistol (+5 points).
- May also choose either a crossbow (+5 points), or a Dwarf handgun (+10 points).
- May carry a shield (+2 points).
- May choose runic items from the Weapons, Armour and Talisman lists (pages 44-47), with a maximum total value of 75 points.
- May have an Oath stone (+20 points).

RUNESMITH
Points/model: 70

	M	WS	BS	S	T	W	I	A	Ld
Runesmith	3	5	4	4	4	2	2	2	9

Equipment: Hand weapon and gromril armour.

Options:
- May be armed with a great weapon (+4 points).
- May carry a shield (+2 points).
- May choose runic items from the Weapons, Armour and Talisman lists (pages 44-47), with a maximum total value of 75 points.

Special Rule
Rune Lore

MASTER ENGINEER
Points/model: 70

	M	WS	BS	S	T	W	I	A	Ld
Master Engineer	3	4	5	4	4	2	2	2	9

Equipment: Hand weapon and gromril armour.

Options:
- May choose either a pistol (+5 points) or a brace of pistols (two pistols, +10 points).
- May also choose a Dwarf handgun (+10 points) and/or a great weapon (+4 points).
- May choose runic items from the Weapons, Armour and Talisman lists (pages 44-47), with a maximum total value of 50 points.

Special Rules
Artillery Master; Extra Crewman; Entrenchment

DRAGON SLAYER
Points/model: 50

	M	WS	BS	S	T	W	I	A	Ld
Dragon Slayer	3	6	3	4	5	2	4	3	10

Equipment: Slayer axes.

Options:
- May choose runic items from the Weapons list (pages 44), with a maximum total value of 75 points.

Special Rules
Slayer; Unbreakable; Loner; Slayer Axes

HEROES

Heroes (Thanes, Runesmiths, Engineers and Dragon Slayers) are the bravest Dwarf warriors in the army, so make great leaders.

The total number of characters you can field in your army can be found on page 48.

*ARMY BATTLE STANDARD

One Thane in the army may carry the Battle Standard for +25 points. This Thane cannot be the army's General.

The Thane carrying the Battle Standard cannot choose any extra weapons, nor can he use a shield. If a Thane is carrying the Battle Standard, he can have a runic standard (no points limit). If he carries a runic standard he cannot carry any other runic item, but can have an Oath stone.

CORE UNITS

This section contains the most common Dwarf infantry types. These units make up the bulk of every Throng. There is a minimum number of Core Units that must be fielded, depending on the size of the army.

There is no maximum limit on the amount of Core Units that can be fielded.

DWARF WARRIORS
Points/model: 8

	M	WS	BS	S	T	W	I	A	Ld
Warrior	3	4	3	3	4	1	2	1	9
Veteran	3	4	3	3	4	1	2	2	9

Unit Size: 10+

Weapons and Armour: Hand weapon & heavy armour.

Options:
- Any unit of Warriors may also carry shields for +1 point per model.
- Any unit of Warriors may also carry great weapons for +2 points per model.
- Upgrade one Warrior to a Musician for +5 points.
- Upgrade one Warrior to a Standard Bearer for +10 points.
- Promote one Warrior to a Veteran for +10 points.

LONGBEARDS
- Units of Warriors can be upgraded to Longbeards for +3 points/model. Longbeards have +1 Weapon Skill and +1 Strength. You cannot have more units of Longbeards than Warriors.
- Longbeard units can have runic standards worth up to 50 points.
- Longbeard units use the Immune to Panic and Old Grumblers special rules.

QUARRELLERS
Points/model: 11

	M	WS	BS	S	T	W	I	A	Ld
Quarreller	3	4	3	3	4	1	2	1	9
Veteran	3	4	3	3	4	1	2	2	9

Unit Size: 10+

Weapons and Armour: Crossbow, hand weapon & light armour.

Options:
- Quarrellers may additionally have shields for +1 pt per model.
- Upgrade one Quarreller to a Musician for +5 points.
- Upgrade one Quarreller to a Standard Bearer for +10 points.
- Promote one Quarreller to a Veteran for +10 points.
- Quarrellers may be additionally armed with great weapons for +2 points/model.

THUNDERERS

Points/model: 14

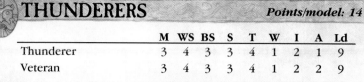

	M	WS	BS	S	T	W	I	A	Ld
Thunderer	3	4	3	3	4	1	2	1	9
Veteran	3	4	3	3	4	1	2	2	9

Unit Size: 10+

Weapons and Armour: Dwarf handgun, hand weapon & light armour.

Options:

- Thunderers may additionally have shields for +1 point per model.
- Upgrade one Thunderer to a Musician for +5 points.
- Upgrade one Thunderer to a Standard Bearer for +10 points.
- Promote one Thunderer to a Veteran for +10 points.
- The Veteran may carry two pistols instead of his handgun at no extra cost.

0-1 RANGERS

Sometimes Dwarf regiments are above ground for years at a time to avenge some outrage against their hold or clan. These regiments are known as Rangers.

A single unit of Warriors, Quarrellers or Longbeards that are armed with great weapons may be upgraded to Rangers at a cost of +1 point per model. These units have the Scout special rule.

Warriors or Longbeards that are upgraded to Rangers can additionally be armed with throwing axes at a cost of +1 point per model.

AFFRONT IN ATHEL LOREN
From the Karak Norn Book of Grudges, 1350

In this year, Grungni Goldfinder agreed to lead an expedition to open up a trade route between Nuln in the lands of the Empire and Parravon, in the lands of Bretonnia. His route passed close by the edge of Athel Loren. Knowing the creatures of the forest to be both capricious and cruel, he avoided the deep woods and followed a path through the ravines at the foot of the Grey Mountains. To avoid incident he bade his followers use only dead wood for their fires.

He had underestimated the vindictiveness of the Elves, however, and they caused the trees themselves to block his path, both forward and back. Without warning, a horde of the Fey appeared at the forest's edge and began to bombard Grungni's followers with arrows. Sending the beardlings back to Karak Norn, Grungni and his best warriors charged deep into the wood to win them time.

May Grimnir curse these ill spirits of the wood for their hatefulness.

SPECIAL UNITS

Special units are extremely specialised troops which appear on the battlefield less often than Core Units.

There is a maximum number of Special Units that can be fielded, and this varies depending on the size of the army.

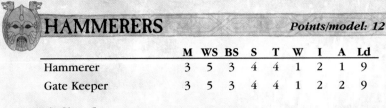

HAMMERERS
Points/model: 12

	M	WS	BS	S	T	W	I	A	Ld
Hammerer	3	5	3	4	4	1	2	1	9
Gate Keeper	3	5	3	4	4	1	2	2	9

Unit Size: 5+

Weapons and Armour: Great weapon, hand weapon & heavy armour.

Options:
- Hammerers may additionally have shields for +1 pt per model.
- Upgrade one Hammerer to a Musician for +6 points.
- Upgrade one Hammerer to a Standard Bearer for +12 points.
- Promote one Hammerer to a Gate Keeper for +12 points.
- Hammerer units can have runic standards worth up to 50 points.

Special Rule
Stubborn; Bodyguard

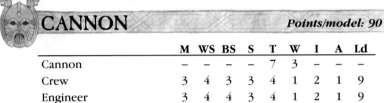

CANNON
Points/model: 90

	M	WS	BS	S	T	W	I	A	Ld
Cannon	–	–	–	–	7	3	–	–	–
Crew	3	4	3	3	4	1	2	1	9
Engineer	3	4	4	3	4	1	2	1	9

Number of crew: 3

Crew's Weapons and Armour: Hand weapon & light armour.

Options:
- You may add an Engineer, equipped with light armour and a hand weapon, who acts as a unit Champion in all respects at +15 points.
- The Engineer may be armed with a handgun at +5 points and/or a brace of pistols at +5 points.

Special Rules
Gunner's Pride, Additional Crew, Engineer has Artillery Specialist

BOLT THROWER
Points/model: 45

	M	WS	BS	S	T	W	I	A	Ld
Bolt Thrower	–	–	–	–	7	3	–	–	–
Crew	3	4	3	3	4	1	2	1	9
Engineer	3	4	4	3	4	1	2	1	9

Number of crew: 3

Crew's Weapons and Armour: Hand weapon & light armour.

Options:
- You may select 1-2 Bolt Throwers as a single Special choice.
- You may add an Engineer, equipped with light armour and a hand weapon, who acts as a unit Champion in all respects at +15 points.
- The Engineer may be armed with a handgun at +5 points and/or a brace of pistols at +5 points.

Special Rules
Gunner's Pride; Additional Crew; Engineer has Artillery Specialist

MINERS

Points/model: 11

	M	WS	BS	S	T	W	I	A	Ld
Miner	3	4	3	3	4	1	2	1	9
Prospector	3	4	3	3	4	1	2	2	9

Unit Size: 5+

Weapons and Armour: Pick (great weapon), hand weapon & heavy armour.

Options:
- Upgrade one Miner to a Musician for +5 points.
- Upgrade one Miner to a Standard Bearer for +10 points.
- Promote one Miner to a Prospector for +10 points. The Prospector may replace his pick with a steam drill for +25 points.
- A unit of Miners may be equipped with blasting charges at a cost of +30 points.

Special Rule
Underground Advance

IRONBREAKERS

Points/model: 13

	M	WS	BS	S	T	W	I	A	Ld
Ironbreaker	3	5	3	4	4	1	2	1	9
Ironbeard	3	5	3	4	4	1	2	2	9

Unit Size: 5+

Weapons and Armour: Hand weapon, gromril armour & shield.

Options:
- Upgrade one Ironbreaker to a Musician for +6 points.
- Upgrade one Ironbreaker to a Standard Bearer for +12 points.
- Promote one Ironbreaker to an Ironbeard for +12 points.
- Ironbreaker units can have runic standards worth up to 50 points.

SPECIAL UNITS

An army may only normally include a single unit of Slayers. However, for each Daemon Slayer or Dragon Slayer included in the army, you may include a further unit of Slayers. This is, of course, constrained by the number of Special units normally permitted in the size of game being played. In a 2,000 point game for example, you can have four Special units in total.

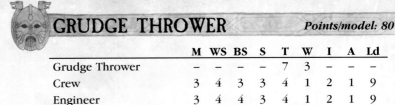

GRUDGE THROWER

Points/model: 80

	M	WS	BS	S	T	W	I	A	Ld
Grudge Thrower	–	–	–	–	7	3	–	–	–
Crew	3	4	3	3	4	1	2	1	9
Engineer	3	4	4	3	4	1	2	1	9

Number of crew: 3

Crew's Weapons and Armour: Hand weapon & light armour.

Options:
- You may add an Engineer, equipped with light armour and a hand weapon, who acts as a unit Champion in all respects at +15 points.
- The Engineer may be armed with a handgun at +5 points and/or a brace of pistols at +5 points.

Special Rules
Gunner's Pride; Additional Crew; Engineer has Artillery Specialist

SLAYERS

Points/model: 11

	M	WS	BS	S	T	W	I	A	Ld
Troll Slayer	3	4	3	3	4	1	2	1	10
Giant Slayer	3	5	3	4	4	1	3	2	10

Unit Size: 5-30

Weapons and Armour: Slayer axes.

Options:
- Upgrade one Slayer to a Musician for +6 points.
- Upgrade one Slayer to a Standard Bearer for +12 points.
- Upgrade any number of Troll Slayers to Giant Slayers for +15 points/model.

Special Rules
Slayer; Unbreakable; Slayer Axes

VENGEANCE IN ATHEL LOREN
From the Karak Norn Book of Grudges, 1352

In this year, Ketil Grungnison and his kin avenged the murder of his father in Athel Loren.

Ketil learned from the men of Bretonnia that the Wood Elves were far less active in winter and therefore waited 'til the snow was deep and the trees were wreathed with ice, knowing that mere weather was nothing to a Dwarf.

He and his party then ventured into the wood and set to hewing down the oldest trees with their axes. Soon enough the Elves came out to fight. This time though, there were no archers, just ranks of thin, pale spearmen. Moreover, they faced Dwarfs armed for war, not peaceful merchants. Led by Ketil, the Grungnisons hewed through the Elvish ranks, sundered their flimsy wooden spears with good Dwarf steel and so claimed a rich blood price for Goldfinder's murder.

Ketil set a great fire of felled trees and Elvish bodies before returning to Karak Norn amid great celebration. Rarely has a grudge been sooner settled. Aware now that we of Karak Norn know their weakness, we expect no more provocation from Athel Loren.

ORGAN GUN

Points/model: 120

	M	WS	BS	S	T	W	I	A	Ld
Organ Gun	–	–	–	–	7	3	–	–	–
Crew	3	4	3	3	4	1	2	1	9

Number of crew: 3

Crew's Weapons and Armour: Hand weapon & light armour.

Special Rule
Gunner's Pride

FLAME CANNON

Points/model: 140

	M	WS	BS	S	T	W	I	A	Ld
Flame Cannon	–	–	–	–	7	3	–	–	–
Crew	3	4	3	3	4	1	2	1	9

Number of crew: 3

Crew's Weapons and Armour: Hand weapon & light armour.

Special Rule
Gunner's Pride

GYROCOPTER

Points/model: 140

	M	WS	BS	S	T	W	I	A	Ld
Gyrocopter	–	4	–	4	5	3	2	2	9

Armour Save: 4+

DOGS OF WAR

Points/model: variable

Dogs of War are mercenary units that you can hire to supplement your army.

You may opt to choose a unit of Dogs of War as a Rare unit in a Dwarf army.

RARE UNITS

Rare units are the scarcest in the Dwarf army, comprising of the more recent war machines which have been invented by the Dwarf Engineers Guild.

In times of great need, a Dwarf Lord may open up his treasuries to hire mercenary units such as Long Drong's Slayers or Ludwig's Wondrous Grenadiers.

HIGH KING
THORGRIM GRUDGEBEARER

Thorgrim is the descendant of the most ancient and noble of all Dwarf lords. The very blood of Grungni flows in his veins and the wisdom of Valaya sits upon his beetling brow. The High Kings have kept the Great Book of Grudges, the oldest and most important of the many Books of Grudges that exist throughout the Dwarf realms. This book, known as *Dammaz Kron*, recounts all the ancient wrongs and deeds of treachery perpetrated against the Dwarf race. Its pages are written in the blood of High Kings, and its tattered parchment is much thumbed and studied.

Occasionally, the Dwarfs have the opportunity to set right some ancient wrong, in which case the High King has the satisfaction of striking out the record in the book. This hardly ever happens as, when it comes down to it, Dwarfs much prefer to hold a grudge rather than let bygones be bygones. Even grudges which have been crossed out can still be read and are never forgotten, but fondly recalled together with the story of how vengeance was finally exacted. Dwarfs are very good at bearing grudges, and Dammaz Kron recounts many episodes of the infamy of other races and of the gods themselves. The Dwarf language has no word for forgiveness, but many subtle variations on revenge, recompense and retribution.

Since an early age, Thorgrim has dreamed of avenging his people and perhaps, one day, to put aside the Great Book of Grudges by striking out every single grudge it contains. Such a thing would be impossible even in a thousand lifetimes, but Dwarfs are determined folk and once their mind is made up they are obstinate. The Great Book of Grudges is Thorgrim's constant companion. He keeps the book by his side night and day, sleeping with its gnarled old pages beneath his pillow, and carrying it about with him in his waking hours. He has managed to strike out several long-held grudges, including winning recompense of 1,000 gold pieces from the Burgomeister of Altdorf for damage done to the reputation of Borin Bullroarer during the Great Altdorf Stampede.

When Thorgrim goes to war (which is often, for there are many dark deeds of infamy to avenge!) he carries the Great Book of Grudges with him. He is borne aloft on the Throne of Power by his four sturdy Thronebearers, and brandishes aloft the Axe of Grimnir. Atop his brow he wears the Crown of Karaz-a-Karak.

THE THRONE OF POWER

For over four thousand years, the Dwarf High Kings have been carried into battle on the Throne of Power. The throne is an ancient wonder and an astounding piece of craftsmanship, a marvel amongst the Dwarfs. The throne normally resides in the cavernous throne room of Karaz-a-Karak, raised upon a massive pedestal of polished stone. Those who would seek an audience with the High King must climb a flight of steep steps as the Dwarf Lord stares down at them imperiously from the massive throne.

Tradition dictates that whenever the King sits down, he must do so on his Throne of Power. To this end, the throne is continually carried around after him as he goes about his daily business. This can be extremely inconvenient, but the Dwarfs are great traditionalists and the High King must be seen to uphold the ancient ways. The throne is borne aloft by four strapping Dwarfs called the Thronebearers. It is a great honour for a Dwarf to be a Thronebearer, for they are also the High King's bodyguard. They follow him all day, and stand by his side wherever he goes. When he is ready to sit they bring his throne for him. When he no longer wishes to walk, they carry him aloft on the throne itself. Only the fittest and strongest Dwarfs are up to this daunting task, and the Thronebearers train rigorously every day. Most of their training involves drinking vast quantities of nutritious Dwarf ale to build up their strength.

The Thronebearers swear a binding oath never to abandon their Lord, and to give their own lives to protect him. Dwarfs take this sort of thing extremely seriously, and to break such an oath would bring lasting dishonour to the oathbreaker's family, descendants and ancestors. In all of Dwarf history there is only one recorded occasion when a Thronebearer, Forkhelm Shiverback, abandoned the High King in battle. His entire family subsequently left Karaz-a-Karak and wandered eastward into the Dark Lands never to return. This terrible shame is not something Dwarfs ever talk about.

It is said that the Throne of Power was made by Grungni himself and that while it endures the Dwarf race will also endure, but should it ever be destroyed then the Dwarf race will be doomed. The throne is inscribed with the great rune Azamar, the unique rune of eternity – a rune so potent that only one of it can ever exist.

THORGRIM GRUDGEBEARER & THE THRONE OF POWER

	M	WS	BS	S	T	W	I	A	Ld
Thorgrim	3	7	6	4	5	7	4	4	10
Thronebearers	3	5	3	4	–	–	3	4	–

Thorgrim can be taken as a Lord choice in a Dwarf army, but will also take up one of your Hero choices as well. He must be fielded exactly as presented, and no extra equipment or rune items can be bought for him.

Points: 780

Weapons & Armour: Thorgrim is carried on the Throne of Power, is armed with the Axe of Grimnir and wears the Armour of Skaldour. He wears the Dragon Crown of Karaz upon his brow, and carries the Great Book of Grudges.

SPECIAL RULES

Thronebearers: The four Dwarfs carrying the Throne of Power make attacks in close combat using the profile above. These attacks do not benefit from Thorgrim's weaponry, and can be aimed at any enemy model in base contact with the throne.

The Armour of Skaldour: This armour is an heirloom of Karaz-a-Karak. This finely-crafted gromril armour bears the Master Rune of Skaldour which confers a 4+ Ward Save, a Rune of Preservation and a Rune of Stone (see page 45). On his throne, Thorgrim has a 1+ Armour Save.

Grungni-wrought Throne: The throne is largely invulnerable to harm, which in itself provides Thorgrim with a degree of protection, and the Rune of Azamar adds to his already heroic resilience. The throne provides Thorgrim with a 5+ Armour Save, and gives him 4 additional Wounds. The Wounds have been included in his profile above.

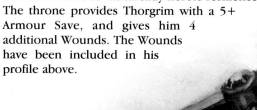

The Great Book of Grudges: This book records every deed of infamy perpetuated against the Dwarfs, scribed in the blood of Kings and infused with the power and anger of its owners. The bearer Hates all enemy. See the Warhammer rulebook for the effects of Hatred. Due to their close proximity to the book, Thorgrim's Thronebearers are also affected by Hatred, as are the members of any unit Thorgrim joins.

Large Target: The throne is a Large Target.

The Dragon Crown of Karaz: Marked with Za, the ruling rune, the Dragon Crown has been worn by the High Kings of Karaz-a-Karak since the hold's founding and is believed to have been brought from the Southlands when the Dwarfs first came to the Worlds Edge Mountains.

The Crown Bears the Master Rune of Kingship.

The Axe of Grimnir: Before Grimnir disappeared into the north he gifted his son, Morgrim, one of his legendary axes. This very axe has been passed down through the generations and it is possession of this artefact that identifies a High King.

The axe bears the Master Rune of Skalf Blackhammer, the Master Rune of Alaric the Mad and the Giantbane Master Rune. The Giantbane Master Rune turns each wound inflicted by the axe into D3 wounds, or D6 if the opponent is a Troll or Giant. There is no other runic item known that combines three master runes in this way.

THOREK IRONBROW, DWARF RUNELORD,
MASTER OF THE WEAPONS SHOPS OF KARAK AZUL

Thorek Ironbrow is a Runelord of the old school. Constant warfare has seen much of the art of the runes lost as holds have fallen to the Greenskins and other enemies. Thorek, however, is as skilled as any Runelord alive today and many would say as any Runelord ever. He has ruled over the weapon shops of Karak Azul for centuries and is a living terror to his apprentices and journeymen who dread his scorn almost as much as they admire his skill and wisdom. Even the sons of kings dare not enter the workshops without Thorek's approval, and many a young would-be Runesmith has found himself back working in the mines for not meeting Thorek's exacting, traditional standards.

It is only fitting therefore that Thorek is the keeper of Karak Azul's Anvil of Doom. Almost alone among contemporary Runelords, Thorek has an understanding of their deeper mysteries. Whilst he has a complete respect for the power of the anvil, he does not fear it, for to him it is a tool on which he can shape and fashion magic like a normal smith would shape iron, gold and gromril.

Although Thorek has no lack of tasks to perform in the Karak Azul workshops, he is prepared to venture forth and take his place on the battlefield. In recent years, Dwarf expeditions have been very successful in recovering ancient treasures from lost and fallen holds. Each such discovery helps keep the precious knowledge of the ancestors alive and that in turn helps ensure that no more holds fall. Indeed it is Thorek's belief that combined with the endeavours of the High King, Thorgrim Grudgebearer and other like-minded kings such as Alrik Ranulfsson, it may yet be possible to retake some of what has been lost.

THOREK IRONBROW

	M	WS	BS	S	T	W	I	A	Ld
Thorek	3	6	4	4	5	3	3	2+1	10
Kraggi	3	4	3	3	4	1	2	1	9

Thorek is the Master Runelord of Karak Azul and, some say, the greatest Runelord alive. He can be taken as a Lord choice in a Dwarf army, but will also take up one of your Hero choices as well. He must be fielded exactly as presented, and no extra equipment or rune items can be bought for him. The cost of his rune items, Anvil of Doom, Kraggi and two Anvil Guards is included in his total cost. See page 30 for the Anvil Guard profiles.

Points: 505

Weapons: The rune hammer Klad Brakak.

Armour: Thorek's rune armour.

THE KLINKARHUN

The core alphabetic runes are called Klinkarhun which means 'chisel runes' and these are the most commonly used and easily recognised. Although the sound of Khazalid does not exactly match the sounds of human speech, the chart here gives the closest approximations. The sounds should be pronounced with force and the 'r' and 'kh' sound in particular are made as if enthusiastically clearing the throat.

Letter	Rune	Letter	Rune
A or I		Kar	
Ak		L or Ul	
Az		M	
B		N	
D		Ng	
Dr or Tr		O	
E		R	
F or V		T	
G		Th	
H		W or U	
K or Kh		Z or Zh	

Num	Name	Num	Name
1	Ong	9	Nuk
2	Tuk	10	Don
3	Dwe	12	Duz
4	Fut	20	Skor
5	Sak	100	Kantuz
6	Siz	144	Groz (also means 'big' in a general sense)
7	Set		
8	Odro	1000	Milluz

RUNE ITEMS

Klad Brakak: Thorek's anvil-headed hammer is a formidable weapon of war as well as a useful tool. In his position as Master of the Weaponsmiths of Karak Azul, he has access to a vast amount of ancient rune lore. From his researches and experiments, he has designed a new rune which he has struck onto his hammer. This rune is unique to Thorek's hammer, Klad Brakak, as he only made it a couple of centuries ago and wants to give it a fair trial before using it again.

In battle it is easy to find Thorek as his hammer shatters armour when it strikes, making a sound like thunder. No Armour Saves are allowed against Klad Brakak and if the target fails its Ward Save (or does not have one) then any armour they were wearing and shield they were carrying are destroyed. This includes magical armour and shields.

In addition, Klad Brakak bears the Rune of Fury which gives Thorek +1 Attack (see page 44).

Thorek's rune armour: This is inscribed with the Master Rune of Gromril (see page 45).

ANVIL OF DOOM

Thorek always brings his Anvil of Doom with him to battle. This works exactly as described in the Special Rules section with the additions noted below:

Master of Ancient Lore. Thorek is so skilled that he can successfully strike runes on the Anvil of Doom with Ancient Power on a roll of 3+.

Assistant at the forge. Kraggi, the best of Thorek's assistants, accompanies him to battle and helps him by preparing some of the runes. Most of the time this is a big help and speeds things up, but occasionally his lack of experience (he's hardly been smithing a century) lets him down and he makes a mistake. Kraggi is treated as a unit Champion and fights with his forge tongs (counts as a hand weapon) and wears a thick leather apron to protect him from the intense heat (light armour).

While Kraggi is alive Thorek may re-roll a failed attempt to strike a rune on the Anvil of Doom. If this extra dice rolls a 1, Kraggi has done something wrong and you should subtract 1 from the roll on the Anvil Miscast table, treating a total of 0 as 1.

JOSEF BUGMAN

Josef Bugman was the most famous Dwarf Master Brewer of all time. To a Dwarf, the art of brewing is a skill as worthy as that of the greatest artisan. All Dwarfs drink vast quantities of ale, and enjoy nothing better than a raucous evening drinking and singing. There are many famous Dwarf ales, and many renowned brewers, but the name of Josef Bugman stands as a paragon of quality. His family originally came from the Dragonback Mountains, and was driven northwards when the mines at Ekrund fell to the Orcs. Some of the Dragonback Dwarfs moved into the Grey Mountains where they founded new strongholds. Later some of these Dwarfs moved into the Empire where they set up as craftsmen and smiths alongside Men.

Josef Bugman's father Zamnil set up in the family trade in the eastern forests of the Empire. He built a stout brewhouse beside the crystal clear waters of the River Sol where it cascades down from the foothills of the Grey Mountains. In order to sell his ale more readily in the Empire, Zamnil took the name of Samuel Bugman, and when his son was born he called him Josef. If Josef Bugman ever had a proper Khazalid name (which is likely), it is not recorded. After his father's death, Josef expanded the business and acquired a considerable reputation for the fine quality and potency of his ale. It was easy for Bugman to ship his barrels on barges down the rivers to the great cities of the Empire where it proved very popular. Soon Bugman's brewery had grown into a small Dwarf settlement and other families came from the Grey Mountains to join him.

Within a few years, Bugman became a prosperous brewing merchant and a reasonably contented Dwarf. With triumphs like Bugman's XXXXXX and the notorious Troll Brew to his name, he was already famous throughout the Dwarf realms. His small community lay well off the beaten track and was usually ignored by any armies or raiders rampaging through the region.

One day Bugman went up river with a shipment of Bugman's Special Brew for the Emperor. As he returned home he saw the smoke gently rising from his brewery among the trees and thought it was about time that the great chimney was swept. When his barge rounded the bend of the river, Bugman saw the smouldering ruins of his settlement. A Goblin raiding party had found the brewery. All the ale had been consumed in a drunken orgy of destruction, the vats were smashed, empty barrels floated on the river and there was no sign of any inhabitants. Every last one of them had been taken off by the Goblins to who knew what fate.

Bugman and his companions swore vengeance on the Goblins for this foul deed and resolved to hunt them down and rescue their kinfolk if they could. The band trailed the Goblins across the Worlds Edge Mountains and into the wilderness beyond. Little was heard of them again except for rumours of the ravages of Bugman and his band, of cunning ambushes and night raids on Goblin camps. Sometimes, the band would suddenly emerge from the wilds, tattered and blood-stained, to join up with a Dwarf army before a great battle with the Goblins. They kept themselves to themselves, huddled around their own campfire, with a strange glint in their eyes and their hands clasped around tankards of precious ale.

JOSEF BUGMAN

	M	WS	BS	S	T	W	I	A	Ld
Josef Bugman	3	6	5	4	5	2	4	3	10

Josef Bugman can be taken as a Hero choice in a Dwarf army. He must be fielded exactly as presented, and no extra equipment or rune items can be bought for him.

Points: 155

Weapons: Bugman is armed with an axe and a crossbow. The axe is a rune weapon, as described below.

Armour: Bugman wears gromril armour and carries a shield.

Bugman's Rangers: Any army including Bugman must include a unit of Longbeard Rangers. These are in addition to the normal allowance of Longbeards and Rangers but do count towards the minimum number of Core Troops choices in the army.

Ranger: Josef is an experienced Ranger and so has the Scout special rule.

Magic Items: Bugman is armed with a rune axe bearing a Rune of Cleaving and a Rune of Fury.

He also carries Bugman's Tankard, a unique family heirloom. Such is the legend surrounding Bugman's ales that any Dwarf drinking from the Tankard will be reminded of the glories of the past, refreshed and restored. In the Dwarf Movement phase, any model in the same unit as Bugman may drink from the Tankard and regain one lost wound. This is not possible if the unit is in close combat.

In addition, any unit containing Bugman and his Tankard will be so refreshed at all times that they are immune to *fear* and *terror*.

The campfire was burning low. Bjarni threw some more wood on it and squatted back down. He did not know the other Dwarfs around the fire as they had come into camp after dark. Bjarni had caught the whiff of ale though, and had brought a couple of burning brands across to get their fire going and be sociable. They were a tight-lipped lot and in the flickering light Bjarni had seen more battle scars and killer's eyes than he had his whole life. He had just about decided to wander off back to his kinsmen when the stranger to his right passed a heavy tankard to him and rumbled,

"Drink, lad. Drink to the past and drink to the morrow's reckoning."

The tankard felt cool in his hand, too heavy for pewter. He could feel the relief-work on it and knew it to be of fine make. Lifting it to his lips he sniffed the heavy aroma of traditional Dwarf ale. It slid down smoothly though, and Bjarni felt his worries for the coming battle melt away. Suddenly he was gulping it down, filled with the well-being that came from the comradeship of his ancestors and the brotherhood of the tavern song.

He looked around him with dream-filled eyes, surprised to note that the tankard was still full. He was about to comment but the owner prised it from his fingers and leaned in close.

"There, now ye can go to battle knowing you have slaked your thirst on Bugman's original brew."

Bjarni's head spun. Was this Bugman himself? Before he could blab out a question his eyes rolled and he slipped slowly backward and began snoring. When he awoke, the blare of the warhorns ringing in his ears, his friends of the night before were gone but his body tingled in anticipation of the battle to come and he hurried to join his kin ready for anything the Grobi had to offer.

REFERENCE

LORDS	M	WS	BS	S	T	W	I	A	Ld	
Dwarf Lord	3	7	4	4	5	3	4	4	10	*Royal Blood*
Runelord	3	6	4	4	5	3	3	2	9	*Rune Lore*
Anvil Guard	3	5	3	4	4	1	2	1	9	*Unbreakable*
Daemon Slayer	3	7	3	4	5	3	5	4	10	*Slayer; Unbreakable; Loner; Slayer Axes*

HEROES	M	WS	BS	S	T	W	I	A	Ld	
Thane	3	6	4	4	5	2	3	3	9	
Runesmith	3	5	4	4	4	2	2	2	9	*Rune Lore*
Master Engineer	3	4	5	4	4	2	2	2	9	*Artillery Master; Extra Crewman; Entrenchment; Gunner's Pride*
Dragon Slayer	3	6	3	4	5	2	4	3	10	*Slayer; Unbreakable; Loner; Slayer Axes*

CORE UNITS	M	WS	BS	S	T	W	I	A	Ld	
Warrior	3	4	3	3	4	1	2	1	9	
Veteran Warrior	3	4	3	3	4	1	2	2	9	
Longbeard	3	5	3	4	4	1	2	1	9	
Veteran Longbeard	3	5	3	4	4	1	2	2	9	
Quarreller	3	4	3	3	4	1	2	1	9	
Veteran Quarreller	3	4	3	3	4	1	2	2	9	
Thunderer	3	4	3	3	4	1	2	1	9	
Veteran Thunderer	3	4	3	3	4	1	2	2	9	

SPECIAL UNITS	M	WS	BS	S	T	W	I	A	Ld	
Miner	3	4	3	3	4	1	2	1	9	*Underground Advance*
Prospector	3	4	3	3	4	1	2	2	9	*Underground Advance*
Hammerer	3	5	3	4	4	1	2	1	9	*Stubborn; Bodyguard*
Gate Keeper	3	5	3	4	4	1	2	2	9	*Stubborn; Bodyguard*
Ironbreaker	3	5	3	4	4	1	2	1	9	
Ironbeard	3	5	3	4	4	1	2	2	9	
Troll Slayer	3	4	3	3	4	1	2	1	10	*Slayer; Unbreakable; Slayer Axes*
Giant Slayer	3	5	3	4	4	1	3	2	10	*Slayer; Unbreakable; Slayer Axes*
Cannon	–	–	–	–	7	3	–	–	–	
Bolt Thrower	–	–	–	–	7	3	–	–	–	
Grudge Thrower	–	–	–	–	7	3	–	–	–	
Artillery Crew	3	4	3	3	4	1	2	1	9	*Gunner's Pride*
Engineer	3	4	4	3	4	1	2	1	9	*Gunner's Pride; Additional Crew; Artillery Specialist*

RARE UNITS	M	WS	BS	S	T	W	I	A	Ld	
Organ Gun	–	–	–	–	7	3	–	–	–	
Flame Cannon	–	–	–	–	7	3	–	–	–	
Artillery Crew	3	4	3	3	4	1	2	1	9	*Gunner's Pride*
Gyrocopter	–	4	–	4	5	3	2	2	9	

DWARF ARMOURY

GROMRIL ARMOUR: 4+ Armour Save

DWARF HANDGUN

Maximum Range: 24"; **Strength**: 4

Rules: Armour piercing; Move or Fire

Superior design: A handgun has a +1 to hit modifier.

ANVIL OF DOOM RUNE EFFECTS

RUNE OF WRATH & RUIN

One unengaged enemy unit anywhere on the table (not an independent character unless it is a large target) takes D6 magical Strength 4 hits distributed as Shooting hits. Affected unit cannot *fly* in its next Movement phase or, if it is not a Flyer, its Movement characteristic is halved until the end of its own following turn. If forced to flee, the unit flees at half speed.

Ancient Power. D3 units are affected, each takes 2D6 Magical Strength 4 hits.

RUNE OF HEARTH & HOLD

Every friendly Dwarf unit may re-roll failed Fear or Terror tests while the note lasts, until the start of the owning player's next Shooting phase.

Ancient Power. All friendly Dwarf units may re-roll Panic and Break tests, and are immune to *fear* and *terror* until the start of the owning player's next Shooting phase.

RUNE OF OATH & HONOUR

One friendly Dwarf unit (not Gyrocopter) may make a normal move (which can be a March or Charge) in the Shooting phase.

Units that move in this way may not shoot in the Shooting phase. Units which rallied earlier in the turn may not make this move.

Ancient Power. D3 friendly Dwarf units will be affected as above.

Grudge Thrower

1) Declare target & guess range (up to 60").

2) Position the 3" template and roll Scatter and Artillery dice.

3) If the Artillery dice is a MISFIRE, refer to Misfire chart in the Warhammer rulebook, otherwise…

   a) If the Scatter dice is a HIT, the stone has struck home.

   b) If the Scatter dice is an arrow, the stone has landed in the direction shown 2", 4", 6", 8" or 10" away from the aiming point as shown on the Artillery dice.

4) All models completely under the template are hit. Those partially under are hit on a 4+.

5) Work out hits at S4. Each wounding hit causes D6 wounds. (A model at the centre of the template suffers a S8 hit). No Armour Save is allowed.

Dwarf Cannon

1) Align the Cannon on the target and guess range (up to 48").

2) Roll the Artillery dice and add the score to the distance aimed. The cannon ball travels forward this distance before striking the ground.

3) If you roll a MISFIRE, refer to the Misfire chart. Otherwise, mark the point where the cannon ball strikes the ground and roll the Artillery dice to establish the bounce distance. All models in the path of the bounce are hit.

4) If you roll a MISFIRE for the Bounce roll, the cannon ball sticks in the ground and does not bounce.

5) Work out hits at Strength 10. Wounding hits cause D3 wounds. No Armour Save is allowed.

THE DWARF ARMY

The following pages show the models of the Dwarf army, grim warriors bearing intricately wrought weapons and armour. As well as guides to the colours of the venerated Dwarf holds, there is information on modelling and painting to help assemble an army of these steadfast, stoic warriors.

65

DWARF LORDS

Lord and Shieldbearers

Lord

Runelord

Lord

Lord

Runesmith

Master Engineer

Master Engineer

Master Engineer

Daemon Slayer

Dragon Slayer

Dragon Slayer

Thorek Ironbrow

Thorek Ironbrow and the Anvil of Doom

The Anvil

Kraggi

Thorgrim
Grudgebearer

Thorgrim Grudgebearer marshals his forces

The Throne of
Power

The Book of
Grudges

CLANSDWARFS

Dwarf Warriors with hand weapons and shields

This regiment features a consistent background colour on its shields, visually tying together all the models in the unit.

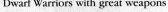

Dwarf Warriors with great weapons

Longbeards

To create this regiment of Longbeards we decided to use the face masks and paint the beards grey, reflecting the Dwarfs' great age.

Dwarf Warriors with hand weapons and shields, Dwarf Warriors with great weapons, Longbeards and Rangers can be made from the Dwarf Warriors Regiment kit.

Quarrellers

Thunderers

Rangers

Rangers are characterised by their great weapons.

Ranger Champion

Quarrellers, Thunderers and Rangers can all be made from the Dwarf Thunderers Regiment kit.

Ironbreakers

Ironbreakers wear gromril armour that is polished to a bright silver colour.

The Musician carries his axe on his back.

A Dwarf Lord leads his bodyguard of Hammerers.

The Hammerers are the King's bodyguard and, to represent their elite status, have a lot of gold on their armour.

We added shields to our Hammerers to protect them from missile fire – the symbol represents the Karaz-a-Karak hold.

These Miners are normally found underground, so are painted in dark, grimy colours.

To make the Champion stand out we chose to give him a blond beard.

Miners

Dwarfs who are unable to fulfil an oath dye their hair orange and tread the path of the Slayer.

An alternative Slayer banner top.

Slayers

DWARF ARTILLERY

Cannon

Crewman

The ammunition is inscribed with runes and curses.

Grudge Thrower

Dwarf artillery arrayed at the Battle of the Hundred Cannons.

Master Engineer

Gyrocopter

Dwarfs avoid making things out of wood as much as possible.

Bolt Thrower

Dwarf artillery pieces are often inscribed with magical runes.

Flame Cannon crewman

Flame Cannon and Organ Gun

COLLECTING A DWARF ARMY

This Dwarf army is a well-balanced force that will do well against any opponent. It has been chosen to a total of 2,000 points, a common size of army for Warhammer battles. The backbone of the throng consists of regiments of Dwarf Warriors, Longbeards and Slayers, and with the addition of the army's general, battle standard and Runesmith, these troops are formidable fighting units that will be difficult for the opposition to destroy. Meanwhile, two units of missile troops backed up by three war machines will pound the enemy, forcing them to close with the Dwarf battle line.

Thunderers
This is a regiment of 16 Thunderers with light armour, handguns and hand weapons. The unit has a Veteran, a Standard Bearer and a Musician. It costs 249 points.

Warriors
This is a unit of 20 Warriors with heavy armour, shields and hand weapons. The unit has a Veteran, a Standard Bearer and a Musician. It costs 205 points.

Longbeards
This is a unit of 16 Longbeards in heavy armour with hand weapons and shields. The unit has a Veteran, a Standard Bearer and a Musician. The standard is inscribed with a Rune of Courage. It costs 247 points.

Thane Kranden Klinkagrul
Kranden carries the army standard. He has a Rune of Stone on his gromril armour and a hand weapon with a Master Rune of Swiftness. He costs 120 points.

Organ Gun
Costs 120 points.

Cannon
Inscribed with a Rune of Reloading. It costs 100 points.

Master Engineer Brugvald
Brugvald has a handgun, a pistol and a great weapon. He costs 89 points.

Grudge Thrower
Inscribed with a Rune of Burning. It costs 85 points.

Quarrellers
This is a regiment of 16 Quarrellers with light armour, crossbows and hand weapons. The unit has a Veteran, a Standard Bearer and a Musician. It costs 201 points.

Hrafn the Runesmith
Hrafn carries a hand weapon and a runestaff with a Rune of Spellbreaking. He costs 95 points.

Warriors
This is a unit of 20 Warriors with heavy armour and two-handed weapons. The unit has a Veteran, a Standard Bearer and a Musician. It costs 225 points.

Thane Volgrim Jormgard.
Volgrim is the Army General. His gromril armour is inscribed with a Rune of Stone. In addition, he carries a shield and a hammer with a Master Rune of Flight and a Rune of Cleaving. He costs 132 points.

Slayers
A regiment of 9 Slayers including a Giant Slayer, a Standard Bearer and a Musician. They are all armed with Slayer axes and cost 132 points.

DWARF HOLDS

Although Dwarfs are all individual in appearance, it is possible to theme regiments and even complete armies by using certain motifs. For example, a hold may be recognised by a prevalent colour or runic design of some kind that most, if not all, the warriors wear. The regiments shown below all hail from specific holds. Even within a single hold, the regiments can vary significantly – for example, three of the units below are from Karaz-a-Karak.

Karaz-a-Karak

Apart from the metal, these Dwarfs of Karak-a-Karak aren't painted a uniform colour. Instead, a number of earthy Dwarf colours are used, namely Regal Blue, Scab Red, Bestial Brown and Catachan Green. These colours are each applied to a different part of each model, such as the cloth and their shields. This gives each warrior a highly individual appearance, while the limited palette of colours still ties them together.

Karaz-a-Karak

This regiment has the same symbol of Karaz-a-Karak on the banner as well as using the same palette of colours as the previous Dwarf unit, although here the similarities end. The banner is painted green rather than blue and, instead of the colours being randomly applied on the unit, these warriors all feature shields with a blue background to the various Dwarf emblems.

Karaz-a-Karak

Gold is the standout feature of this Longbeards regiment, also from Karaz-a-Karak. The individual models are painted red, blue, brown and green in the same way as the other Dwarfs from this hold, giving each warrior an individual appearance. However, the striking Shining Gold colour applied to the majority of the unit's metal details helps to make the regiment stand out from the other examples from this hold.

Karak Hirn

Unlike the warriors of Karaz-a-Karak, and indeed the other regiments in this spread, the army of Karak Hirn is painted a single colour: green. However, in typical Dwarf fashion, the greens used to paint the models are slightly different – Dark Angels Green and Camo Green. The other unifying elements on this regiment are the colours used for the shields: Boltgun Metal with Shining Gold for the details.

Karak Kadrin

This regiment from Karak Kadrin has a strong red theme – the banner, shield and helmets are all painted Scab Red. The matching shield symbols on the rank and file troops are painted Brazen Brass, a colour used for the details on the rest of the unit. To make the red theme appear even stronger, the rest of the colours on the warriors are muted greens and browns.

Karak Izor

The shields of this unit are painted Dwarf Bronze all over and this colour is applied to the warriors' helmets, the banner top and their wristbands. The rest of the colours used to paint this unit are even more muted than those normally favoured by Dwarfs – only greens and browns, without any red or blue. This makes the bronze theme even stronger on the unit.

PAINTING BEARDS

In painting the Dwarf regiments shown in this book we've used lots of different colours for the beards. Here's a selection of painting schemes you can use.

Dark Brown
- Bestial Brown basecoat.
- Apply a wash of Scorched Brown.
- Highlight with Bleached Bone.

Light Brown
- Bleached Bone basecoat.
- Apply a wash of Flesh Wash.
- Highlight with Bleached Bone & Skull White.

Black
- Chaos Black basecoat.
- Highlight with Codex Grey, followed by a highlight of Fortress Grey.

Grey
- Codex Grey basecoat.
- Highlight with Fortress Grey, followed by a highlight of Skull White.

Orange
- Basecoat with a mix of Scorched Brown & Blazing Orange.
- Highlight with Blazing Orange, then highlight with Bronzed Flesh.

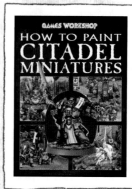

For everything you need to know about painting Citadel miniatures.

The Throng of Karaz~a~Karak

SHOWCASE

Some gamers like to convert their models with additional parts from the Warhammer range to give that personal touch. Others use Classic models from Games Workshop's back catalogue, often applying painting techniques and colours that show off their skills. On this page are examples of these different approaches.

Bugman's Rangers – Classic miniatures

Dwarf Lord conversion
by Owen Branham

King Alrik of Karak Hirn
painted by John Addison

Thunderer conversion
by Joseph Wiltshire

Engineer conversion
by Joseph Wiltshire

Troll Slayer conversion
by Victoria Lamb

Dwarf Lord by Mike Dodds.
This model has been painted
without using metallic paints.

Longbeards – Classic miniatures